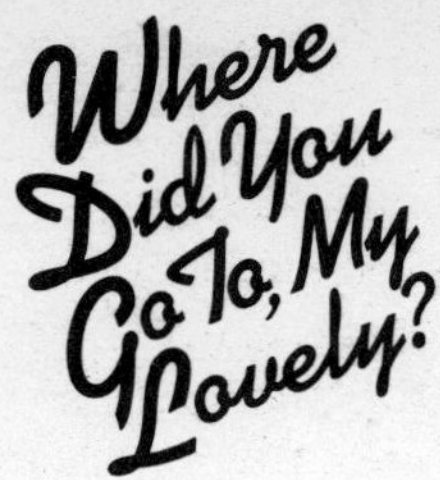

'There was a time when I used to get so frustrated about music. But my missus would say: "Don't worry, you're out of it now." And I am. I mean, I've got a good job that brings me twelve grand a year plus a company car and all the perks . . .'

Cliff Bennett

'Oh darling, those boots! The only reason I ever wore them was because my legs were so bloody awful.'

Twinkle

'Arthur just came up one day and said: "Look, I can't make it anymore. My heart's not in it and I'm getting too fat . . ."'

Ray Phillips of the Nashville Teens

FRED DELLAR

Where Did You Go To, My Lovely?

**The lost sounds
and stars of the sixties**

A STAR BOOK

published by
the Paperback Division of
W. H. ALLEN & CO. Ltd

A Star Book
Published in 1983
by the Paperback Division of
W. H. Allen & Co. Ltd
A Howard and Wyndham Company
44 Hill Street, London W1X 8LB

Copyright © 1983 by Fred Dellar

Printed in Great Britain by
Cox & Wyman Ltd, Reading

ISBN 0 352 313749

My thanks to Norman Divall, Peter Jones, Spencer Leigh, Dave Dee, Dave Hadfield, Leon Campadelli, Terry Noon, Johnnie Francis, Tony Meehan, Al Clark, Pete Frame, Barry Collings, Brian Gannon, Frankie McGowan, Hal and Ray Carter, *NME* and all the folk who are doing such a great job at *Goldmine*.

Without you all, I'd still be looking at a blank sheet of paper.

Contents

Foreword

WRITING A BOOK about the stars of the sixties seemed such a good idea at the time. Each week I'd received scores of queries from *NME* readers asking: 'Whatever happened to Stevie Marriott?', 'Where is Dave Clark these days?' and such like. There appeared to be so much interest in the fate of others who had apparently ready, steady, gone, that I eventually got around to tracking fifty or so of them down. The ones who had been neglected, I mean. None of your actual Stones, Kinks, and Who-people – groups who have lacked nothing in the way of publicity since the days of Edison (well, Edison Lighthouse, maybe!). And I certainly didn't want to write about The Beatles – not after deliberately turning down offers from four different publishers to pen tomes on the Fab Four in the wake of John Lennon's death. Instead, I decided to amaze everyone with my findings on such folk as Billie Davis, The Honeybus, Love Affair, The Equals and The Four Pennies, acts that had accrued a fair number of hits during the sixties but, for one reason or another, had run out of steam as the seventies arrived.

I repeat, it seemed a good idea at the time. The only problem was that most of the acts on my hit list didn't cooperate – they just wouldn't stay forgotten! Dave Dee, after years on the other side of the show-biz tracks, began running around with Dozy, Beaky, Mick and Tich once more. Brian Poole and Jet Harris started playing gigs for the first time in yonks, Helen Shapiro recorded her first British album since 1965, Herman returned from self-imposed exile to appear in the London production of *The Pirates of Penzance* and poor Billy Fury grabbed the headlines in the saddest possible way.

Additionally, most of the others began turning up on such TV nostalgia shows as *Unforgettable* and *Greatest Hits*, thus ensuring that my brainchild would never emerge as the complete 'whatever happened to' affair it might have been.

No matter. Good luck to them all, I say. After all, over the years, the people whose lives fill this particular publication have provided me with many hours of musical pleasure. Also, when I began my bout of research, I discovered just how friendly most of them had remained. Even when I turned up on their doorsteps or rang their homes to ask sometimes personal questions, virtually everyone assisted in every possible way – only one or two offering a polite 'thanks, but no thanks'. So, if the flurry of renewed interest in the stars of the sixties has resulted in most of my case-histories now having upbeat endings instead of the tear-in-the-eye conclusions they might have received only a few months ago, then so be it.

Like the great majority, I prefer happy endings all the time.

Fred Dellar

NO SMOKING

Cliff Bennett & The Rebel Rousers

CLIFF BENNETT CAME from Slough. Well, somebody has to come from Slough. He sang with local bands and skiffle outfits during the fifties and formed The Rebel Rousers in 1961. They came on really trendy – snazzy tartan jackets and everything. They also had all the right connections. For, after signing to play the Star Club, Hamburg, they met Brian Epstein and signed with NEMS. A down-the-line R&B outfit, with Bennett usually donating gritty, soulful vocals over a background of booting saxes and wailing organ, they joined Parlophone, the record label that housed The Beatles, and went Top Ten in 1964 with 'One Way Love'. In 1966, they did even better with a Beatle number, 'Got To Get You Into My Life', produced by a real live Beatle, Paul McCartney. After that, the band never really managed to get back on the right rails again. Even a cover of Lennon-McCartney's 'Back In The USSR' failed to make much of an impression. Eventually the band split and Bennett, now long-haired, formed a band called Toe Fat, which made a couple of albums in the early seventies but is now best remembered for the sleeve of their first album, which ranks among the most unpleasant in the whole history of rock. There were other attempts and other failures: first with a band called Cliff Bennett's Rebellion, which surfaced for a CBS album in 1971, and, in 1975, with a much-vaunted outfit called Shanghai, a band that also provided employment for Mick Green, once guitarist for Johnny Kidd and The Pirates. By 1976 Cliff Bennett's love affair with rock music was over and he retired from the business, a somewhat disillusioned man.

'I got burnt so many times,' he says. 'The final straw was Shanghai. We were with a company called Thunderbird Records. They had massive financial backing but went through all the money in about six months. Then the directors of the company – who included Mick Green – sold the group up the river, as far as I'm concerned. They signed with President Records and didn't tell me with whom they'd done a deal until the very day we went to meet President's Ed Kassner. I simply refused to work with him. I told him he'd only paid The Equals thirty quid a week even when they'd had five chart hits. He counterclaimed that he'd supported the band for ten years. Eventually he just said: "If you walk through that door, you're finished." And I said: "I'd rather be finished than work for you – I'll just go out and get a real job." Which is what I did. The following day he got an injunction to stop me signing or recording for anybody else. Later, I fought it in court and, in my eyes, I won the day because he had to pay all the costs and I got my contract back. But the whole thing really spoilt my appetite for the music business.

'Earlier I'd had problems with Les Reed's Chapter One Records. I got an advance from that company and when they went broke, the Official Receiver came gunning for me. I had to tell him that he could have all the tracks that I'd done plus any money that I had left. I've still got those tapes. I've got lots of stuff that never came out – it's all piled up in my garage.'

Cliff Bennett is still happy to talk about his past bands and ex-Rebel Rousers like Frank Allen, who went on to join The Searchers, keyboardist Roy Young, who later led the moderately successful Roy Young Band, and Chas Hodges, who is now half of the highly popular Chas and Dave team.

'What I really hate is the people who keep ringing me up and promising me things. John Gunnell, who used to manage many of us in the old days, came back from America a short while ago and asked if I wanted to do an album with Geno Washington, Georgie Fame, Zoot Money and Chris Farlowe. I had to tell him that the scene had changed somewhat but he still maintained he'd be able to do things. Later he came back and admitted that he hadn't had much joy at all. Record companies had just kept slamming doors in his face. Then, I've always had people calling me and saying: "I can do this for you". At one time it really got on top of me.'

Bennett's been a sales executive with an aviation firm for some time now, though he has been known to nudge his way into music on rare occasions. 'About three years ago I went over to the Star Club, in Hamburg, and spent a couple of days there doing a special anniversary show with people like Lee Curtis, PJ Proby and Wee Willie Harris. We worked in front of about two thousand people and I'm told that the club was sold out two weeks prior to the event. Then there was the *Heroes And Villains* show, at Hammersmith, last year. I didn't want to do that but Dave Dee explained that it was all for charity – all the money went to handicapped children – so I went on and it was fantastic! Afterwards they said they could have sold enough tickets to fill up the place for a further three nights!'

The voice of Cliff Bennett also reaches into your living rooms some evenings. 'That's right. I've been doing adverts for television – I did all the voice-overs for Carlin Black Label. I work for a company called Crocodile Music who do a lot of ads and I even did a record for them recently. It's a sort of spin-off from the Carlin Black Label thing but it's not been placed anywhere. I don't get a chance to do such things these days. I'm off to Newcastle tomorrow and won't be back till the end of the week. At the end of the month I'm going out to Zimbabwe, after which I'm due to go to Dubai. You see, I'm all over the place now. There was a time when I used to get so frustrated about music. But my missus would say: "Don't worry, you're out of it now." And I am. I mean, I've got a good job that brings me twelve grand a year plus a company car and all the perks. All I really do musically these days is maybe get up at a dinner and dance and have a blow with the band, if I know the boys!'

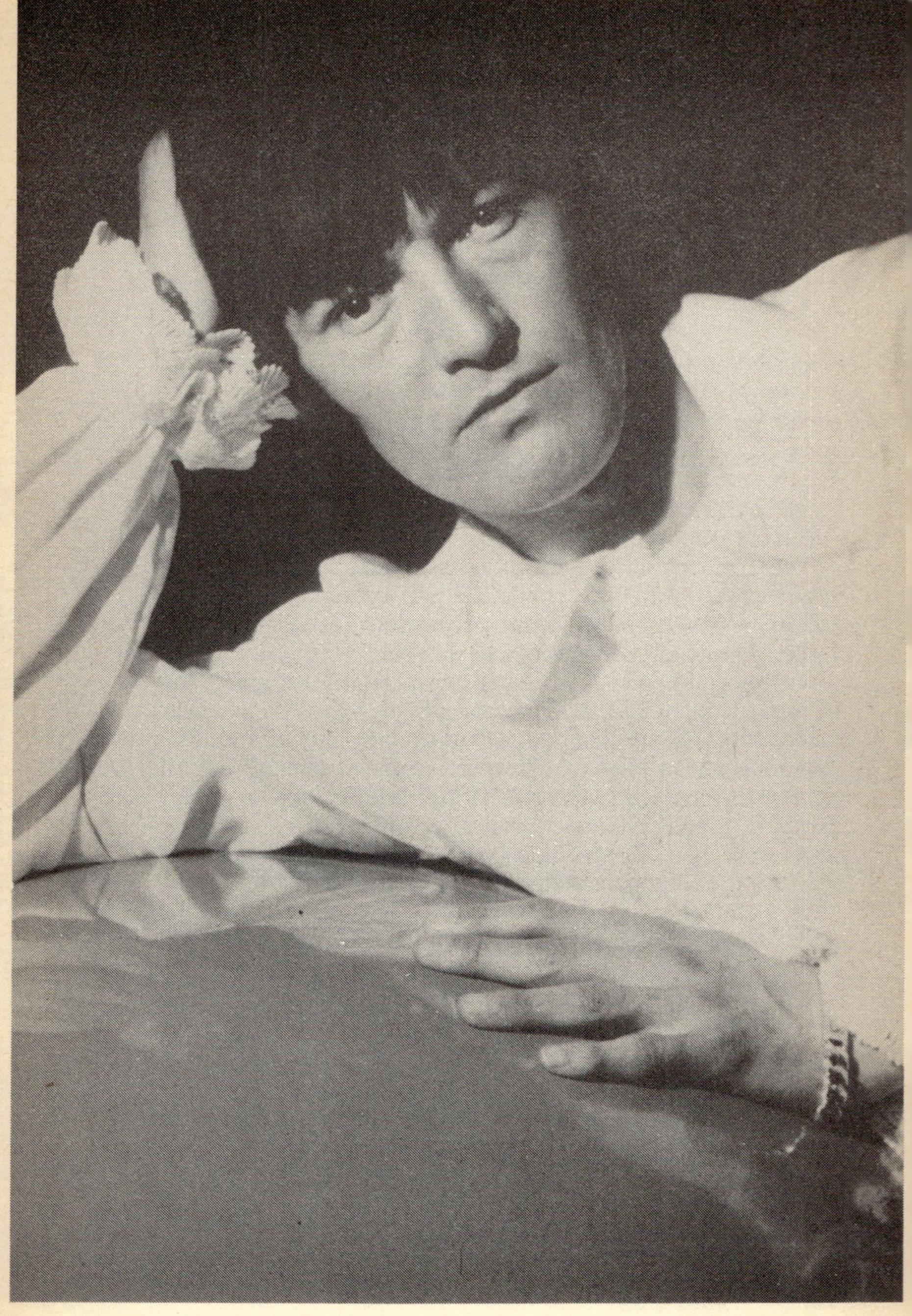

Dave Berry

Dave Berry was – and still is – the most charismatic of them all. He had a hypnotic style that was all his own – a way of slithering round props like a snake exploring a monkey tree, a way of handling a mike that reminded you of Vincent Price folding a silk scarf in readiness for his next Corman-sponsored strangling.

Many years later, Alvin Stardust tried the Berry style on for size and found that it worked to his advantage with the audiences of the seventies. But it was Berry, bless his socks – which were black, like every other part of his apparel – who was the true originator of the serpentine approach. At least that's the way it's going down in this particular book.

A Yorkshireman, from Sheffield, David Berry Grundy started out as an R&B singer, leading a band called The Cruisers. In 1963 he had a hit with a version of Chuck Berry's 'Memphis, Tennessee', following it up with renditions of Arthur Crudup's 'My Baby Left Me' and Burt Bacharach's 'Baby It's You', both of which did pretty well. Then he switched styles, recording a ballad called 'The Crying Game', which featured an innovative guitar solo courtesy of Jimmy Page. A haunting release, it went Top Five, as did 'Little Things' in 1965, and 'Mama' in 1966. His records didn't sell after that – not in Britain, anyway – and, according to one rock encyclopedia: 'ruffled by the wind of change that blew through the pop scene in 1967, he disappeared onto the Northern club circuit.'

'But I've never been part of the Northern club scene,' says Berry, who currently has a full date book. 'I've just come back from France and Belgium where I've been playing universities. A lot of my work is in Europe – during the seventies and even now I do two or three tours every year in Belgium and Holland. I've done lots of other things too – song festivals in Yugoslavia, a seven-week stay in Rhodesia, that's when it was *still* Rhodesia, and even a London Lyceum gig with Adam And The Ants a couple of years ago.'

The realisation that he's become something of a cult figure among young rockers brings considerable pleasure to Berry.

'It's nice because my audiences are getting younger. I think a lot of bands are looking back to the sixties these days. The Monochrome Set did some of my stuff a couple of years ago and when I did the 'Heroes And Villains' concert in 1982, a member of one of the newer bands said in the *Melody Maker* that he liked what I did. And that's great – much better than somebody who was brought up in the sixties saying the same thing. It means that I am making some impression on young people. I still retain an enthusiasm for music. I see as many bands as I can – Siouxsie And The Banshees, for instance, they're a great visual act. And I still buy records, mainly chart albums by people like ABC, Echo and The Bunnymen and A Flock Of Seagulls. I'm not one of those people who just look back on the sixties as a golden era. You have to remain interested otherwise everything becomes merely a routine and what you do onstage wouldn't mean anything. I suppose my act these days is a reflection of the sort of music I've liked over the years. I do rockabilly things like "Bring My Cadillac Back" and Carl Perkins' "Boppin' The Blues". Then there's Janis Joplin's "Mercedes Benz", Dylan's "Knockin' On Heaven's Door" and that weird Gene Vincent track, "Get It". I've never lost my roots. I was an R&B singer to start with – though I got a little sidetracked.'

Many fine musicians have worked with Dave Berry during his career. Joe Cocker used to sit in with the original Cruisers at Sheffield gigs during the early sixties, John Paul Jones was another who sat in alongside Jimmy Page on some of the Decca sessions. Eric Woolfson, the musical mastermind behind The Alan Parsons Project, wrote, arranged and produced 'Movin' On', Berry's 1972 single for CBS, while other sessions have found him working with 10 CC's Eric

Stewart and also Chas and Dave.

'Ray Davies of The Kinks wrote a song called "This Strange Effect" for me, some years ago,' Berry will tell you, neglecting to mention that his recording of the number turned out to be one of the biggest sellers in Dutch music history. 'John Verity (ex-Argent and Phoenix), who's produced a couple of albums for Saxon, was once a member of my backing band. In fact, John and I have been trying to sort out some new material because it's possible we might get together in a recording studio shortly, though nothing's definite. In all honesty I haven't recorded *that* much since the sixties. And some of the things that I've done have never appeared in Britain. The Chas and Dave sides, for instance, were only released in Germany.'

Now resident in a house set amid England's Peak District – 'Not far from the M1, so I can get to gigs, but still well into the country' – Dave Berry is a happily married man and has been so for fourteen years.

'I met my wife in Amsterdam, when I was doing gigs over there, so we met because of my work. It wasn't as if we had met as childhood sweethearts or anything like that. I think in those sort of circumstances things are more likely to go wrong when you're faced with an entirely different lifestyle. Happily my wife doesn't mind me making trips all over the place. In fact she wouldn't like it if I was here all the time. So I just carry on creeping about onstage. But at home I'm quite normal. Honest!'

Mike Berry

ALL ENQUIRIES AS to the whereabouts of Mike Berry ended abruptly in the summer of 1980 when, following a hiatus of some seventeen years, his name once more graced the British Top Ten.

Berry's first tilt at stardom really got under way in 1961 when cutting records that had connotations of death seemed a reasonable way to make it into the charts. It was then that he and The Outlaws, a band basically utilised as a session outfit by producer Joe Meek, recorded 'Tribute to Buddy Holly', a song penned by Geoff Goddard (who also wrote John Leyton's 'Johnny Remember Me' and Heinz's 'Just Like Eddie') and helped themselves to a Top Ten hit by so doing.

The Outlaws had originally been The Stormers but the image-conscious Meek had changed their name in order that all promotional work could be given a 'western angle' – the band riding into towns aboard a stage-coach and so forth. They began recording and touring with Berry on a regular basis though they still continued making records of their own. It was their liaison with Berry that brought in the shekels, however, and in early 1963, the singer and his wayward band – who at one point found themselves the subject of a *News of the World* exposé, following a flurry of flour-bomb throwing activity between gigs – notched up yet another Top Ten single with 'Don't You Think It's Time', which, in turn, led to an appearance in the film *Live It Up*. But the year also saw Berry and The Outlaws eventually heading their separate ways, the band moving off to back Gene Vincent for some months before their penchant for looning got the better of them and they were given the elbow by the black-clad rocker.

Somehow, though, with the work situation worsening along with their reputation, they stuck things out until early '65, by which time, Mike Berry himself had faded into oblivion.

Later, he recalled: 'In the two years of my three hit records, I was earning £450 a week gross, £120 net – good money in those days. But with the coming of the groups, I was swept aside like an old leaf. By 1967, all my money had gone. Some grotty pride stopped me drawing unemployment benefit and my wife supported me on her earnings as a hairdresser.'

Berry still continued to make club appearances and occasionally cut the odd single or two for labels like Penny Farthing and York. Also, aided by his actor brother Peter, he moved into the theatrical profession, gaining work with repertory companies or doing stints in pantomime. Following some bit parts on TV he also discovered something of a gold seam in the world of advertising. He was in demand as a photographic model and frequently appeared in TV commercials.

A 1976 version of 'Don't Be Cruel', backed by a re-run of 'Tribute To Buddy Holly', provided a fillip to Berry's recording career, the disc proving a hit in Belgium and Holland and a healthy seller in Britain, despite a lack of BBC airplay. 'If the record does become a hit here,' Berry said at the time, 'The adverts for bowls of soup and cups of coffee will probably have to take second place.'

But, though comfortably off from his advertising earnings – which enabled Berry, his wife and two children to move into an Edwardian house in South London – he had to wait until 1980 and the singalong success that was 'The Sunshine Of Your Smile' before he became a full-blown pop star once more. 'The Sunshine Of Your Smile' was masterminded by Chas Hodges, bassist with The Outlaws throughout the whole of the band's existence. Nowadays he's one half of Chas and Dave and doing very nicely, thank you.

Some of his fellow Outlaws have acquitted themselves rather well too – especially Ritchie Blackmore, guitarist with the band from 1963 onwards. A founder member of Deep Purple, he's currently leading his own heavy metal outfit,

Rainbow, and presumably enjoying the profits of such hits as 'Since You've Been Gone' and 'All Night Long'. Bobby Graham, the original Outlaw drummer, has made a couple of solo singles along the way but spent most of his time as a sessionman. Mick Underwood, his replacement, has since played with just about everyone in the business, his appearances with Episode Six during 1967–68, a band featuring vocalist Ian Gillan, leading to a full-time gig as skin-basher with Gillan until a throat ailment forced the band's mainman to call a halt to the unit's activities at the close of 1982.

Berry, in the interim, has logged no more massive hits, though such singles as 'If I Could Only Make You Care' and 'Memories' have done pretty well for him. And he's also gained a few fans through regular appearances in the *Worzel Gummidge* and *Are You Being Served?* TV series, not to mention his 1982 panto season at the Lewisham Empire and further telly-ad spots for Blue Riband wafers and OSL Holidays.

Certainly his bank manager approves.

Pete Best Four in 1963

Pete Best

 Some reckon Pete Best to be the unluckiest figure to ever emerge from the whole sixties' music scene. And in some ways he was. For if any one person ever got around to filling in the winning line on the rock'n'roll pools and then failed to post it, then that person was Pete Best.

Things started out just fine for him. After all, he was good-looking and bright. His mum, Delhi-born Mona Best, owned a large, fourteen-roomed Victorian house in the West Derby area of Liverpool – something else which worked to his advantage. When he and some of his mates decided to start a coffee club at which bands could play, he was able to use the cellar in his own home. And a fella named John Lennon came round to help with the decorating. It was Lennon's group, The Quarrymen, who played the club's opening gig, in August, 1959. Even up to its opening day, the venue had no name. Then Mona Best, deciding that the place looked like a set out of Charles Boyer's *Algiers* movie, dubbed it The Casbah. And the name stuck.

Pete became a drummer and formed an outfit called The Blackjacks. Then The Quarrymen, who'd become The Beatles, offered him their drum chair for the duration of a German trip. He stayed for two and a half years.

The crunch came in August, 1961, just after George Martin had offered The Beatles a contract with EMI's Parlophone label. Manager Brian Epstein asked Best into his office one day and told him he had some bad news. 'The boys are replacing you with Ringo Starr,' he said. Quite literally, he'd been nosed out.

When the news got out, there was a furore at Beatle gigs.

John, Paul and George got involved in punch-ups with Best supporters. Crowds clamoured around The Cavern yelling 'Pete for ever, Ringo never'. Best, meanwhile, moved on to become drummer with Lee Curtis' All-Stars, the November 15 edition of *Merseybeat* reporting that his fame was such that several girls had taken to sleeping in his garden, just to be near him!

As The Beatles took their first steps towards becoming millionaires, The Lee Curtis All-Stars began establishing an enviable reputation on the Liverpool music scene. But, when the record companies came in waving their cheque books, Best and his new mates always seemed to get left out in the cold. By 1963, the drummer had moved on to form his own outfit, The Pete Best Four, cutting a Decca single, 'I'm Gonna Knock On Your Door', which did virtually nothing. A trip to New York followed: Best led a group known as The Pete Best Combo and recorded some tracks that didn't materialise into records. Thoroughly disillusioned, he returned home to Liverpool and took a job in a bakery.

'It was a case of having to,' he told *Goldmine* magazine. 'I stayed there for about twelve months and then a job with the government came up and I've been there ever since. It's a job-oriented position. We call it Employment Services. It's finding people jobs.'

Mona Best still lives at the house in West Derby. 'The Casbah closed in 1962,' she recollects. 'It was a popular coffee club at a time when there were lots of similar little clubs in Liverpool. Then, in 1962, scores of licensed clubs opened up in the city. They came in with something of a bang and all the coffee clubs took a severe knock. I still live in the same place though – they'll have to get me out of here with a shovel – but these days my youngest son Roag, who has a punk band, uses part of the cellar to practise in. He and the band, What For, rehearse down there. They've even got a four-track recording studio too, though the rest of the place has all my old junk in it. Roag's one of my three sons, the others being Rory and Peter. Roag's a drummer and I think Peter had a lot to do with that. He looks up to Peter and says that if he can only be as good as his brother then he'll be

happy. Peter's working at his old job, in the employment
office in Garston, these days. His wife's name is Cathy and
they have two girls – Biba, who is nineteen, and Bonnie, who
is fourteen. They're both very grown-up now. There was a
time when Peter was thinking of emigrating to America. But
it took so long for the green visa, the permit, or whatever it
was, to come through that all the plans he made and all the
contacts that he had seemed to disappear, simply because
people couldn't wait that long. You see, he wanted to go over
with his family. He could have left them behind and lived a
bachelor existence but he didn't want to do that. So he's still
in Liverpool and helping to push Roag. Roag's also taking
drumming lessons. He really wants to read music. Something
Peter couldn't do – he only played by ear. The young
drummers are very good these days. So good that I think that
Peter and drummers of his era would find it very hard to cope
with the younger boys who are coming up.'

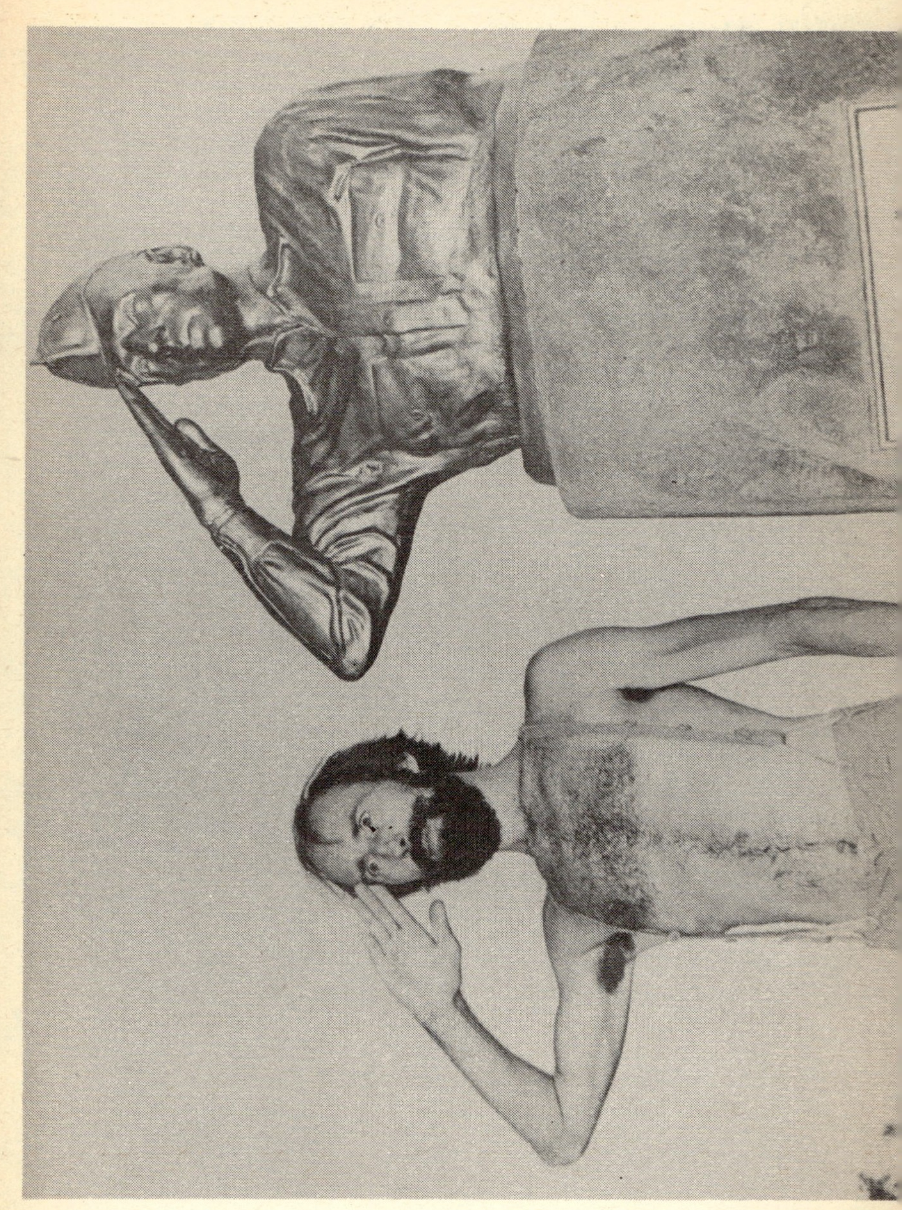

Arthur Brown

He seemed like a genuine nutter. At a Windsor Jazz Festival gig, clad in long robes, he made his entrance dangling from the arm of a crane. And every time he rendered 'Fire' in his Screaming Jay Hawkins voice, he set his dishevelled barnet ablaze just to make things a little more realistic. His band was known as The Crazy World Of Arthur Brown and its members were equally unpredictable, two of them ending up in mental institutions after one particularly mind-blowing American tour.

It was coincidental that 'Fire' came out in mid-1968, in the very week that a blaze at Olympic Studios, Barnes, was grabbing the headlines, a blaze that involved The Rolling Stones, who were working at the studios. Maybe that very coincidence helped gain the single a plentiful number of radio plays. Or maybe it was just because it was a great, driving rock record – which it was. Either way, 'Fire' got well aired and well bought too. Within weeks the charts were set ablaze as the single by the Whitby-born, East London schoolteacher scorched to Number One.

But, though The Crazy World contained some outstanding musicians in drummer Carl Palmer, later of ELP and Asia, and keyboardist Vincent Crane, who went on to form Atomic Rooster, 'Fire' proved the band's lone hit. And being admired by such theatric-rock lovers as Peter Gabriel and David Bowie didn't help pay the bills. In 1969, Arthur Brown announced that he was quitting. After a breathing space, he began working with an experimental band and then formed Kingdom Come, a band which, by their third album, had moved on to become totally electronic, using a rhythm box instead of a drummer for live appearances.

Ahead of the times Kingdom Come may have been. Ahead

of their debtors they were not. Before long Brown was forced to embark on other projects, providing a solo album called 'Dance', which didn't add up to very much, and grabbing a role as a manic preacher in The Who's film presentation of *Tommy*, a part which some saw as type casting.

The late seventies found Arthur Brown moving further and further into the realms of electronic music. He performed live with Klaus Schulze in Paris during 1977 and, a couple of years later, embarked on a forty-date tour with the German synthesiser player. He also spent time working on a number of albums for Schulze's own label.

At the start of the eighties, Brown decided to head for America and chance his luck there. A deal with a Houston record label was offered and Brown settled down in Texas, awaiting developments. Unfortunately the deal fell through and Brown was forced to earn his living as a carpenter. He still lives in West Austin, Texas, with his American wife Selena, and is still a carpenter, though he recently recorded a remarkable anti-nuclear concept album called 'Requiem', just to prove that old avant garders never die nor completely revert to making tenon joints.

'It represents different ways of looking at nuclear war,' he says of the album which, again, is highly electronic. 'It's not something with a heavy message. There's a conversation between an ant and a cockroach who meet after the world's blown up and there's another song about human potential — about what mankind can do if they don't blow themselves up. The same subject, seen different ways.'

It's likely that an Arthur Brown Band will be on the road sometime during 1983, a band featuring synth player Scott Morgan, who appears on 'Requiem'. 'I'll also be using video and theatrics in the show,' he says.

Probably it'll all be a few years ahead of its time. Then, that's something Arthur Brown's always had to live with. Maybe if he'd burned himself to death back in 1968, he would have become a legend and rock buffs could have spun tales of how great he would have been had he survived.

Ever noticed just how many musicians are adjudged great *after* they're dead?

Dave Clark Five

I REMEMBER Dave Clark smiling.

He always seemed to be smiling. If you turned the TV set on when any mid-sixties pop show was in progress, inevitably, Dave would be there, sitting behind a drumkit, his teeth flashing in the spotlights.

These days he still has a lot to smile about. He resides in a Mayfair penthouse flat and has the sort of bank balance most record companies would be chuffed to have to their credit. A careful man. And he admits as much.

'Even when the band had their first big hit, we stayed on as resident band at the Tottenham Royal for just £20 a week. People kept coming up and telling us that we should become fully professional, and maybe at that time we did lose a lot of money by not immediately going on the road.'

The band – The Dave Clark Five – was originally a fun outfit formed to raise funds for a local football club. But, by 1961, after a few changes in personnel, they'd found favour on the Mecca ballroom circuit. This, in turn, led to a couple of records for Pye's Piccadilly label – both of which flopped. Clark then used some of the proceeds from his work as a film stuntman to record further tracks that were leased to EMI.

Clark, a part-time musician right up to the time that he appeared on *The Ed Sullivan Show* in 1964, was born in Tottenham, London. It was at the Tottenham Royal that the band first came to the attention of an EMI A&R man. Thus it was that when the DC5 eventually made their breakthrough, the publicists touted the band as having invented the 'Tottenham Sound', a rival to Merseybeat. Presumably, if they'd been viewed at one of their earlier Basildon Locarno

shows, their music might have been termed Basildon Bop. Record companies are funny like that.

The Five, then Clark (drums), Mike Smith (vocals, keyboards), Denis Peyton (sax), Lenny Davidson (guitar) and Rick Huxley (bass), had their first EMI-Columbia single released at the end of March, 1963. And it flopped. The follow-up didn't. A cover of The Contours' 'Do You Love Me?', it edged its way into the Top Thirty. Next came the big one. Titled 'Glad All Over', it was so big that it even swept The Beatles' 'I Want To Hold Your Hand' from the top of the charts.

One immediate result was that the band, whom Clark not only led onstage but also managed, quit their residency at the Royal and handed over the gig to The Migil Five, an action that sparked a fan riot at the dancehall, gaining the DC5 acres of press coverage.

Hotter than White Hart Lane at Cup time, the North Londoners made four more British hits that year, including 'Bits And Pieces' and 'Can't You See That She's Mine'. They also had eight hits in America, where they became the first British beat group to tour, preceding The Beatles by several weeks.

Subsequently they became massive in the States, where they toured many times and appeared on countless TV shows, these appearances including a score or more of *Ed Sullivan* dates. Meanwhile, back in Britain, they starred in the 1965 John Boorman film *Catch Us If You Can*, playing a group of stuntmen (typecasting for Clark). Later that year they appeared before the Queen at a Royal Command Performance. Recordwise, their success continued, the title song to *Catch Us If You Can* and 'Everybody Knows' reaching the Top Ten in the UK during 1965 and 1967 respectively. And in America, where the inhabitants had been hooked on smiles even before the advent of Doris Day, DC5 singles continued to sell as if Howard Hughes was buying them all personally. Clark's rendition of 'Over And Over' became Number One in 1965, a year in which the DC5 enjoyed four other major hits in America.

It was in 1967 that Dave Clark finally announced that

enough was enough. 'We just decided to call it a day. I mean, the first world tour is exciting and so is the second. But after a while it just isn't any fun any more. We went to the States about thirty times, played every state except Alaska – but all we ever saw was the inside of planes and locked hotel rooms. While we were onstage, everything was fine. I loved performing – but it's the rest of it that destroys you. After a while you begin to lose your identity. So we decided to stop touring and maybe just do TV and records. After all, we'd always gone down well on TV. It was at this time that I decided to attend the Central School of Speech and Drama, which Sir Laurence Olivier was running then. I did three years there, full-time, right through from first thing each morning. I did Shakespeare and things like that there, all very hard work for me. But the thing was that I'd always wanted to direct. And the best directors are generally actor-directors – they know from experience just how far they can push people in order to get the best out of them. Previously I'd thought of myself as an actor and, frankly, our first film was well-received. Though after viewing it, I realised that my performance left something to be desired.'

The occasional DC5 record still continued to emerge and, thanks to releases such as 'Red Balloon', 'Good Old Rock'n'Roll' and 'Everybody Get Together', the band remained a Top Ten proposition right up to early 1970. Clark never did get around to directing any films but he continued making records for a while, cutting tracks under the title of Dave Clark And Friends, which continued to surface right up to 1975. When he finally stopped recording, somebody, somewhere, estimated that Clark had sold in excess of thirty-five million records worldwide. Which wasn't at all bad.

For a while Clark and Mike Smith masterminded the career of singer John Christie. Smith later moved on to team with ex-Manfred Mann singer Mike D'Abo as Smith And D'Abo, for a while, before edging into the world of radio jingles, where he remains to this day, earning an excellent living through thirty-second long boosts for such products as Sunblest bread. Rick Huxley runs a musical equipment shop in South-East London. Lenny Davidson owns a number of antique stores and Denny Peyton was last heard of running a property firm.

So what's Clark himself up to these days?

'I've been working on a musical for the past two years. It's called *Time* and is very much a now thing. I hope that it'll play both London and Broadway but the likelihood is that it'll first emerge as a kind of concept album, with lots of stars on it.'

Dave Clark as a challenger to Tim Rice and Andrew Lloyd-Webber? It seems that's the way things may yet turn out.

So much for the future. How about the past? 'I wouldn't have missed the sixties for the world. I feel that I was lucky to have spent my time in the sixties, there was such an optimism about things then. I didn't care for some of the music of the early and mid-seventies. A lot of it turned out a bit clinical maybe, because the studios had all gone twenty-four track and bands were able to perfect every detail right down to the last drum fill. All our stuff and most of The Beatles things were just four-track. If we made mistakes, they often showed. But it was these very imperfections that sometimes lent the music its character. The coming of punk did a lot to put things right again and there's a lot of good music around once more thanks to that punk thing of '76. Meanwhile it's crazy how our old songs keep turning up. Kiss did "Anyway You Want It" a little while back and then Joan Jett did "Glad All Over". It's nice to know we're still remembered.'

Jess Conrad

IF NOTHING ELSE, Jess Conrad will always be remembered for making some of the worst pop records ever to come out of the sixties. No less than three were selected for the 'World's Worst Record Show' compilation released by K-Tel in 1979, while DJ Kenny Everett voted 'This Pullover', an early Conrad offering, the worst-ever pop record he had *ever* heard! High praise indeed!

Back in the days when a dollar was a dollar and there were at least four to the pound, Conrad, then known as Gerald James, was a star-struck fifteen-year-old who worked for a stainless steel vessel merchant in Kingston, Surrey. 'I had to stand inside the large urns pressing a great flat weight against the wall of the urn while somebody on the outside belted it into shape with a mallet. Then, one day, I saw a man lose a couple of fingers in the machinery and I decided then and there that I had had enough of that particular job!'

Eventually, following a stint with his dad's flower-selling business in Shepherd's Bush, the six foot one good-looker became a film extra and rep player – his first singing role coming in a Hornchurch presentation of *Jack And The Beanstalk*. It was St Valentine's Day, 1959, that brought the big break – the part of a rock'n'roll singer in a TV play called *Rock-A-Bye Barney*. The fan mail rolled in and, along with it, the offers of work. One came from producer Jack Good who told him: 'Jess, you can't sing but you have a certain teenage quality. You start work on Monday in ABC-TV's new rock show *Wham!*'

At the end of the series he was voted the show's most popular singer. Not that this popularity was reflected in record sales. His first hit, 'Cherry Pie', was only a mild one. Number Thirty-nine in the midsummer charts of 1960, in fact. But it was a start. By February of the following year he was a *real* pop star, with a Top Twenty record all of his own. Titled 'Mystery Girl' it was dedicated to a girl who passed by his Dulwich home each morning. T'wasn't much – but it *was* a hit. And a tour in the company of Gene Vincent did his reputation no ill at all. In one music paper poll he was actually voted top male singer, above Cliff Richard.

His record success quickly petered out, however. There was just one more mild tilt at the charts – with 'Pretty Jenny' in 1962, after which the Conrad career became mainly tied to the theatre and TV. 'I'd always wanted to be a young actor who sang – someone like Tab Hunter or James Darren,' he once claimed, 'but in this country it seems you've either got to be a rock'n'roller *or* an actor.'

So Conrad became an actor – one who turned his hand to musicals, whenever good parts became available. He turned up everywhere, in films like *The Golden Head*, *Hell Is Empty* and *The Assassination Bureau*, on TV (yes, he did appear in *Crossroads*), on radio and in touring companies. He even made a few records from time to time, though none of them gave him any remote tinge of hope in the pop star revival stakes.

Music still formed part of his life. He took over from David Essex in the touring version of *Godspell* and was cast as Joseph in the Andrew Lloyd Webber–Tim Rice musical *Joseph And The Amazing Technicolor Dreamcoat*. Then, in 1976 he began touring with a band called The Hollywood Rock Machine, presenting a show titled *Jess Conrad Pays Tribute To The Kings Of Rock'n'Roll*. Well-liked among fellow pop singers and musicians, he roped together a bevy of talent for an EMI single, 'Save It For A Rainy Day', the disc being produced by former Marmalade member Junior Campbell, other contributions being made by Dave Dee, Mike Batt, Troy Dante and Chip Hawkes of the Tremeloes. Again though, the record failed to make the charts and, after a brief appearance in The Sex Pistols' *Great Rock'n'Roll Swindle* movie, Conrad returned to the world of stage musicals, appearing in *Leave Him To Heaven* in 1979, also playing in a revival of *Joseph And The Amazing Technicolor Dreamcoat*, at London's Vaudeville Theatre during 1980–81 and at Sadler's Wells in 1981–82.

One of the chief mourners at Billy Fury's funeral in 1983, Jess Conrad has always retained his links with the world of rock and pop and maybe, just maybe, one day he'll come up with another hit single. In the meantime he seems happy enough to be carrying on with his acting and minding not in the least whenever some memento of his earlier career becomes the victim of some Everett diatribe.

'Kenny really did me a big favour when he played my early discs and said that they were amongst the worst ever made,' he explained to a *Music Week* reporter. 'In the early sixties everyone was singing about the girl next door and other mundane subjects and songs had ridiculous titles like "Cherry Pie" and "Kicking Up The Leaves". Funnily, "This Pullover" had a beautiful Italian melody but it also had excruciating English lyrics and it was those that Everett was making fun of. Anyway, the radio exposure he gave the records was good for me because it reminded people that Jess Conrad was still around.'

David And Jonathan

DAVID AND JONATHAN? But all they had was two hits in six months before they did their impression of the great oozlum bird, I hear you say.

In a way that's right. But theirs is not such a tale of fizz and flop – I mean, when you've chosen a name nicked from a biblical tag-team you have to expect a few miracles. So what we have here is a tale of winners – and it starts in Bristol, where the twosome left school at the age of fifteen, each separately wending their way through a variety of everyday jobs but ever edging towards the music biz.

After working with the Kestrels, a Bristol group, they teamed up in 1965 both as performers and songwriters, one of their compositions, 'You've Got Your Troubles', proving a massive hit for The Fortunes. Almost overnight they became something of a hit factory turning out winners for Freddie And The Dreamers, Petula Clark and various others. But when they climbed into the 1966 charts with a record of their own they did it utilising a Beatles song – 'Michelle'. They had one further major hit that year with 'Lovers Of The World Unite'. After which their only hits were those which they supplied to other acts. Still they pulled good money at their club gigs – around £500 a night. But in mid-1968 they quit performing as a duo and began concentrating on the backroom activities of the music world – composing, jingle-writing, producing and sessionwork. Reverting to their real names – Roger Cook (Jonathan) and Roger Greenaway (David) – they formed a company called Cookaway Music and really cleaned up in 1970 when 'Home Lovin' Man', 'My Baby Loves Lovin'' and 'Good Morning Freedom', all songs in which Cook and Greenaway had a hand, went Top Ten for Andy Williams, White Plains and Blue Mink respectively.

Not surprisingly they walked away with the Songwriters Of The Year award when the Songwriters Guild handed out their annual plaudits at a get-together held during 1971.

Cook must have been doubly pleased with the way that 'Good Morning Freedom' charted, for not only did he help write the number but he also performed it in his capacity as a member of Blue Mink, a part-time band put together towards the end of '69.

Blue Mink proved a winning idea right from the start. In their first year, the band – with Roger Cook and Madeline Bell handling most of the vocals – made a tremendous impact with their recording of 'Melting Pot', following it with 'Good Morning Freedom', 'Our World', 'Banner Man' and 'Stay With Me', most of these numbers being products of Cookaway Music.

Cook and Greenaway were writing separately by this time. 'When we wrote together, things tended to get a bit samey,' Roger Cook later admitted. But still the songs were published bearing both of their names. And the twosome dreamt up hits at a prolific rate, stopping only to supply the world of advertising with jingles that they either wrote or performed (sometimes both), these including ditties for Typhoo, Bass, Woodpecker Cider and many others. They supplied Coca Cola with the well-known 'It's The Real Thing' earbender. 'I used to have time to be at home with my wife, watching my three kids grow up,' Cook complained, 'But during recent months everything has exploded and I can hardly find an hour to myself.'

Apart from his usual flow of multifarious activities Cook had also embarked on a solo vocal, cutting a number of singles and albums for EMI's Regal Zonophone label during 1972–73. For once, however, his luck ran out and though he turned in such excellent albums as 'Meanwhile . . . Back At The World' and 'Minstrel In Flight', both packed with Cookaway songs, nothing charted.

He still continued to supply highly commercial material for others though – and in 1975 he gave a song to The Rimshots called '7654321 Blow Your Whistle', which did pretty well. But, surprise, surprise, it contained no label credit for Roger Greenaway. It seemed they had, after years together, decided to end their songwriting partnership.

By 1976 Cook was ensconced in Nashville: he had decided to begin a whole new career in country music. And, against all odds – for in Music City even the studio cleaner is a singer-songwriter with his eye on the main chance – he became accepted as one of the best song-shapers in Tennessee.

He's remained there to this very day, doing very nicely, thank you. If you don't believe, then ask singers like Don Williams and Crystal Gayle, for whom he has penned Number One country hits, published by his own company, Cook House.

After Cook's departure for the States, Roger Greenaway ploughed on in his usual industrious fashion, one of his more lucrative chores involving songwriting and record production for The Drifters, the American group to whom he gave a new lease of life. 'Roger really knows me,' said Johnny Moore, The Drifters' lead singer, in 1974. 'He knows my sound. I think he sings similar to me – with a high-pitched voice. So he knows what I hear, knows what I can do.'

One way or another, Greenaway did manage to revitalise the group, who hadn't landed a British hit since 1967. After he teamed with the foursome, in 1972, a series of winners simply streamed off the record presses, the partnership logging some eleven hits in four years, most of them being Top Ten entries. Currently, Roger Greenaway is still riding high. In January, 1983, he was appointed chairman of the British Performing Rights Society, an exalted position in the UK music business.

'I don't get so much time to write songs these days,' he'll tell you. 'In fact, I've only had the time to write a couple of songs a year during the past two years. I've done some production and gotten involved with lots of jingles, some of the commercials I've provided being for such companies as British Gas, Asda and Allied Carpets. I still see Roger Cook – I visit him about twice a year. He's amazingly successful now and the funny thing is that we should both end up writing American country music hits for Crystal Gayle – I wrote "It's Like We Never Said Goodbye", her 1980 Number One. As for the old days, when we were David and Jonathan – well, I'm always happy to hear someone play "Lovers Of The World Unite" on the radio though it seems funny when they refer to you as a golden oldie! I've never regretted giving up performing however – there were so many other things that I wanted to do.'

Billie Davis

'SHE STANDS THERE. Not quite as tall as you might have thought. And you notice how pretty she seems. Thick ropes of dark hair frame her face. Hidden behind the recording screens, waiting for her cue. As fragile as glass. Billie.' So read Michael Aldred's brief sleeve note to Billie Davis' 1970 album, merely titled 'Billie Davis'.

She was attractive, too: dark eyed and dark haired. And she could sing more than a bit – though you'd have never known it from her first hit record, 'Will I What?', a comedy item on which she played stooge to Mike Sarne. A few months later, in February 1963, the one-time Carol Hedges, an 18-year-old from Woking, Surrey, made her solo way to the top with a cover of The Exciters' 'Tell Him', a Top Ten single that immediately established her as a singer of considerable potential. Billie became the girl-friend of bass-guitarist Jet Harris and was with him in the car-crash which to all intents and purposes finished his career. Billie too suffered severe injuries in the crash, breaking her jaw. Understandably, her career had to take a backseat for a while, never actually getting back on course again until 1968, when her version of 'I Want You To Be My Baby' flickered around the lower edges of the charts.

The 1970 album, produced by *Ready, Steady, Go* stalwart Aldred, was a strong one and augured well for a further revival in the Davis fortunes. Nothing happened in Britain, though in Spain, where 'I Want You To Be My Baby' remained in the charts from January through to November, Davis became a major star, gaining a TV series and numerous hit singles.

Billie Davis, in 1983, hasn't changed that much in appearance. She's a mite chubbier perhaps, but her dark hair is styled in the way that you remember from way back when. Her voice is in good nick too. Better than ever, in fact. She plays a tape she made with George Williams, once leader of The Tymes, and the twosome's voices intertwine in the same miraculous way that Marvin Gaye's and Tammi Terrell's once did.

'Really I want to get more into writing nowadays,' Billie explains. 'I've written some things with the help of Pierre Tubbs [writer and producer of such hits as Maxine Nightingale's 'Right Back Where We Started From'] – it was Pierre who suggested that I should write, start putting all of my ideas down on paper. It's only over the last couple of years that I've really managed to concentrate on this aspect of my career. Prior to that, for about ten years, it's been all backwards and forwards to Spain. That's because of "I Want You To Be My Baby", which was originally a jazz thing by Lambert, Henricks and Ross. We [the 'we' being Billie, producer Aldred and arranger Mike Vickers] wondered if it was possible to get away from the jazz feel and edge it into more of a disco thing. And it worked. Actually, the record ran into a lot of bad luck here in Britain – Decca went on strike and no records got into the shops. Which was unfortunate because we had every conceivable TV show, radio and everything. So it only got to around 28 or somewhere. But it took off everywhere else and opened the doors to Spain and all the Spanish-speaking countries in South America. They didn't know who I was at first though – when I arrived, they thought I was a boy! Since then I've travelled to places like Rio and Argentina and found myself on all sorts of amazing shows. One bill I shared with a bullfighter and a flamenco star! I learnt the language – once they gave me a script in Spanish and I said, "I can't do this", though somehow I *did* and got through the show – and nowadays, when I write, I try to do Spanish versions as well.'

Billie's released quite a few singles in Britain during the past few years – on labels such as Philips, UA and Magnet, though none of them has done much to re-establish her as a

name artist. She still plays a fair number of gigs here – at
venues like Blazers, at Windsor, and in 1982 she began
touring with comedian Harry H. Corbett.

'It was sort of a variety thing. Harry would do his spot and
then I'd sing a little. Then maybe we'd do something
together, like a version of "Makin' Whoopee" with different
words. I was learning all the time, Harry was such a
professional and I learnt a lot from him. But when he died,
well that was the end of that. I was also asked to appear on
the sixties revival show at Hammersmith last year but when
Dave Dee phoned I said I couldn't do it because I was about
seven months pregnant. I've since had a little girl, her name is
Celyn Sian. It's a Welsh name because she was actually born
in Wales. I'm not married now, I don't think I could live with
one person all the time any more. I was married before, and I
have a ten-year-old son, Simon, by my previous husband. He
and I are still friends but I just find it difficult to be around
any one person all the time. The way things are I'm very
happy.'

She still has a kindly word to say about Jet Harris and
remembers his attempts to make a comeback with some
sadness. 'After the car crash – which happened on the way
back from a show which I'd been doing – the agents kept
saying to Jet that it'd do him good to get back to work. He
had all sorts of contracts and there was a lot of pressure on
him to resume playing. At his Edmonton comeback concert
he was great during rehearsals but when he got on stage he
just couldn't handle it. I don't really know what it was with
Jet. All I do know is that when he had something to drink, he
became sort of schizophrenic – and he really didn't need very
much to drink. I used to lock him in his dressing room during
shows so that he couldn't go out and be tempted by other
people in the show who might come up and say, "Have a
drink and you'll feel better." Once he went back and worked
on *Ready, Steady, Go!* but he felt so bad because of the
accident – his hair was still growing back on the place where
he'd had all the stitches – that he just ran out of the studio.
We were watching television at home, when suddenly there
was a knock at the door and there was Jet! I looked at him

and looked at the television and said: "But you're supposed
to be on there!" He had a tremendous talent, though, and
was Britain's most popular musician at the time of the
crash — which is why it was such a big story.'

Spencer Davis Group

IT MIGHT HAVE been Davis' group in name. But without the vocals, guitar, keyboards and other skills of Stevie Winwood, it's doubtful if you'd be reading about The Spencer Davis Group right here and now.

Winwood was, and is, a remarkable musician. A proficient provider at all the best jazz licks at the age of fourteen, he and his bass-playing brother Muff teamed up with guitarist Davis and drummer Pete York to form The Rhythm And Blues Quartet, an outfit that gigged solidly around Midlands clubs. They became The Spencer Davis Group and turned professional in 1964, just around the time that their debut single, 'Dimples', came out.

Powered by Stevie Winwood's blackest of black-sounding vocals, the band built on their reputation during the next few months, gaining airplay with records like 'I Can't Stand It', 'Every Little Bit Hurts' and 'Strong Love', nudging into the lower reaches of the charts. And when they did eventually hit, they came on strong, with two Number One records in a row, 'Keep On Running' – a record which proved that Christmas '65 didn't have to be *all* turkeys – and 'Somebody Help Me', an Easter '66 success. Both songs were penned by Jamaican writer Jackie Edwards, who also supplied their next hit, 'When I Come Home'. The group, with Stevie Winwood now on organ, then began writing their own chart material, and two originals, 'Gimme Some Lovin'' and 'I'm A Man', proved to be Top Ten moneyspinners.

Stevie by this time, *was* the band. Not only was he one of the country's most distinctive singers and musicians but he also wrote much of the band's material and was also responsible for its overall sound. No one was surprised, therefore, when he nipped off to form Traffic in early '67, his brother also quitting to become an A&R man with Island Records. Equally, few were surprised that The Spencer Davis Group failed to ever gain a major chart record after the Winwood exodus. It seemed that the heart had been torn out of the band.

Nevertheless, it continued to survive in reasonably buoyant manner for a while. Davis and York were joined by keyboardist Eddie Hardin and guitarist Phil Sawyer, this line-up producing 'Time Seller', which just edged into the Top Thirty, and also contributing to the soundtrack of *Here We Go Round The Mulberry Bush*, a film that also featured music by Traffic.

More changes followed, Sawyer being replaced by Ray Fenwick. And still the band clung on to its reputation as a chart outfit, a single, 'Mr Second Class', climbing as high as 35 in early 1968. After that, nothing seemed to work. Hardin and York moved off to form a moderately successful duo. Their replacements, Nigel Olsson and Dee Murray, only stayed around for a short while before opting to become part of Elton John's regular back-up squad. Eventually even Ray Fenwick looked for a solo career and Davis, with no band and no recording contract, was forced to move to the USA in pursuit of a new career.

'I felt I needed a break,' he said later, 'time to reflect and think things through.' In the States he did sessionwork and played Californian coffee-houses in the company of a fellow Brummie, folk-musician Pete Jameson. After two years he reappeared in Britain once more – to make a final stab at re-establishing The Spencer Davis Group in the company of ex-members York, Hardin and Fenwick, along with newcomer Charlie McCracken, formerly bassist with Rory Gallagher's band Taste.

Tour dates poured in – good ones, at universities and colleges, plus some at high class venues on the Continent. There were also two new albums, 'Gluggo' and 'Living In The Back Street', both for the thriving Vertigo label. But despite Davis' attempts to come to terms with the seventies, the main requests at most shows were for 'Keep On Running', 'Gimme Some Lovin'' and all the old hits.

'We enjoy playing them,' Davis said at the time, 'and people have always asked us to do them. When Pete and Eddie were together they were always asked to do the old Spencer Davis numbers and it was the same for Pete Jameson and myself. We just couldn't leave them out.' The band couldn't continue to exist on faded dreams, however, and following some further changes in personnel, the band split for the last time, Spencer himself eventually heading back to America.

Today, over a decade and a half on from the time when the Winwoods began carving out their own careers, the original Spencer Davis Group is remembered with some affection. In 1978 Island released a 'Keep On Running' EP which sold extremely well, while in 1982 that same Jackie Edwards song, performed in the Spencer Davis manner, turned up in a TV advert for Andrex toilet tissue!

Stevie Winwood's career is well-documented. After several fruitful years with Traffic and the short-lived supergroup Blind Faith, years which, oddly enough, only produced three hit singles, 'Paper Sun', 'Hole In My Shoe' and 'Here We Go Round The Mulberry Bush' – all during 1967 – he moved on to embark on a low-profile but financially rewarding career as a solo artist eventually resulting in such massive-selling albums as 'Stevie Winwood', 'Arc Of A Diver' and 'Talking Back To The Night'. In 1981, the year that 'Arc Of A Diver' was released, Stevie was the second biggest record-selling artist in America, quite a feat for a musician who, in recent times, has been something of a recluse, preferring to spend his life working on his Gloucestershire farm than touring with a band. He has his own recording studio – Netherturkdonic Studios – built next to his home and there is able to concentrate on his music, sometimes working eight hours a day, six days each week. But, as he explained in a *Goldmine* interview: 'There are always jobs to be done on the farm and I'm a great believer in doing mindless physical things for relaxation. When I'm not in the studio I like to get out in the fresh air and dig a hole or something. Moving bales or fencing or logging – there's always work to be done because I don't employ enough people to do it.'

'Steve sometimes comes up to London and goes round with me, hearing various new bands,' says Muff Winwood, who's currently head of A&R at CBS Records. 'He doesn't get a lot of chance to hear much in the way of new sounds, so he always takes the opportunity to do the rounds with me whenever he's in town. Some of the bands we hear, he hates. But there are others that he's liked.'

Muff became A&R man at Island Records at the time that company switched from being merely a reggae label with a few other irons in the fire to being a substantial force in the music world.

'Prior to that, Island had mainly licensed lots of things out. Their first *real* group was Traffic. I worked for them for about five or six years then went out as an independent record producer, though I also ran Island's Basing Street Studio at the same time. We had an agreement – I would work as an independent producer as long as I brought all my acts to record at that studio.'

Among the acts Muff has produced over the years can be numbered Sparks, The Sutherland Brothers and Quiver, The Bay City Rollers, Mott The Hoople, The Fabulous Poodles and Dire Straits.

'Since being at CBS, which I joined some four-and-a-half years ago, I've signed Shakin' Stevens, Altered Images, Adam and The Ants, Bonnie Tyler and quite a few others. I still see Pete York now and again. He and his wife run a restaurant in Lambourne, an upper-class place where they get all the horsey fraternity coming in. He still plays and does a lot of work on the Continent. Funnily enough, only last night I turned on the TV and there was Pete playing drums behind some girl singer! Spencer – he's still in the States. He's working for a big video company, one that does videos for people like Fleetwood Mac and other major acts. Incidentally, I hear that Stevie is in America right now, working on an album with the people from Chic. This summer he's putting a band together and is setting out on a world tour.'

Finally, one remembrance of his days as bassman with SDG. 'The great thing about coming up in the sixties was that you could make money while you were still a semi-pro musician. This meant that you could take your time developing. Nowadays it's difficult to do that. I think myself lucky that I was part of a rock and roll band just at the time when the bubble was really exploding.'

Dave Dee, Dozy, Beaky, Mick And Tich

DAVE DEE LIVES in a three-storey house in North London. It's an older property but one which in estate agents' terms is 'a desirable residence', modernised throughout and decorated in a tasteful manner, the walls hung with a multitude of excellent prints. One glance around and it's evident that though Dee quit singing with a chart band in September, 1969 and only resumed his activities in recent months, he's fared far from badly in a financial sense. A one-time policeman – legend has it that he was the first copper to appear on the scene following the road accident that killed Eddie Cochran in 1960 – Dee (real name David Harman) became the leader of The Bostons, a band that could be found gigging in the Salisbury area of Wiltshire during the early sixties. One night they played a gig with the then hit-parading Honeycombs and wiped the floor with them. After which, Howard and Blaikley, who'd masterminded The Honeycombs' success, also became responsible for the affairs of The Bostons. They renamed the band Dave Dee, Dozy, Beaky, Mick and Tich, merely using the nicknames by which lead guitarist Ian Amey (Tich), rhythm guitarist John Dymond (Beaky), bassist Trevor Davies (Dozy) and drummer Mick Wilson already possessed. Using Howard and Blaikley's songs – all of them totally commercial, DDDBM&T moved impressively into the charts, claiming success with their second single, 'You Make It Move', which reached Number Twenty-six in late 1965, while their third disc, 'Hold Tight', a real tub-thumper, gained them a Top Ten hit in March, 1966.

A totally stagy band, dressed to kill in best Carnaby Street fashion and larger than life in terms of song presentation, DDDBM&T ran riot through the charts during 1966–1968, logging such spectacular hits as 'Hideaway', 'Bend It', 'Save Me', 'Touch Me, Touch Me', 'Okay', 'Zabadak', 'The Legend of Xanadu', 'Last Night In Soho' and 'Wreck Of The Antoinette'. The biggest of these was 'Legend Of Xanadu', an item which featured Dee in ultra-macho guise, his bullwhip-cracking routine sending TV viewers flooding into the record shops, thus giving the band a UK Number One. In Germany, it was much the same: during 1967, DDDBM&T became even bigger than The Beatles and The Rolling Stones.

It was in 1969 that things began winding down. Two of the band's singles, 'Don Juan' and 'Snake In The Grass', struggled to make the twenty-third spot in the charts and Dee decided that the time had come for a change.

'I went solo and had a record out called "My Woman's Man". It was about the time that Phonogram, who released the single, decided to change their distribution. It proved a real balls-up. They switched all their records from one depot to another and people just didn't know where they were. Richard Barnes had got "Take Me To The Mountain" into the Top Forty and my record was also up there. But no further records went into the shops for some weeks and by the time the record company had got its act together, the radio stations had ceased playing the single. After that, with my first record not being as big as it might have been, things got harder. I made two or three more singles but they didn't get the radio play that the first had got. That's when I decided to call it a day.' Dee planned to go into acting but didn't pursue the idea – 'What I should have done was to go into rep, like Adam Faith did, earning around £15–£20 a week while I learnt a craft. But after you've struggled to the top and taken about ten or twelve years to do it, you don't really want to go right back to the beginning again.'

So Dee went into cabaret, making more money in two-and-a-half years than he'd made in all his years with the band. Then, at the same time, he was offered both the role of Kenickie in the London production of *Grease*, and the post of label manager at Atlantic Records. He went to Atlantic, later being appointed A&R manager of Warner Brothers, the parent company. Dee signed several important acts to the company and proved so successful that some German backers offered to finance a label of his own – Double D. Unfortunately the label foundered during what was a slump period in the industry and Dave Dee moved on to Magnet Records in 1982, where he spent a short period as head of press and promotion before opting out.

'The band had gone on in the meanwhile as DBM&T, their first single, "Mr President", getting caught up in the same distribution problem that I'd encountered. After two years they packed it in – Mick Wilson leaving the band for good. All the others went on and did various things for a while. Beaky played with various bands, Tich played with The Troggs for a few months. And it was when he was playing with The Troggs, in Germany, about five years ago, that everyone in the audience suddenly recognised him and started shouting out for "Legend Of Xanadu" – right in the middle of The Troggs' set! He recognised that there was still an audience for the band and got the boys back together again – but with a new Mick. Since then, they've been DBM&T once more, though Beaky and Tich have worked in a band called Mason and also in a band called Tracker, just as a break from the DBM&T thing.

'In December, 1981, I was asked to tour Germany with the band but said "No". Then came an offer to visit Germany for one day, all expenses paid, put up at a good hotel and all that. So I said that if I could have a three-day holiday in Hamburg with my lady – all expenses paid – I'd do a gig with the band. And that's what happened. I hated doing the show. The PA equipment was nothing like that which we'd used in the sixties and I thought the sound was terrible. But the audience seemed to enjoy themselves and the agent sent me all the reviews, which were quite complimentary. So I did some further dates in May, 1982, and quite enjoyed them. Since then we've done another tour and have another lined up. Maybe I'll continue working with the band for, say three months of the year, and spend the rest of the time working with my own management-promotion company. In the wake of the *Heroes And Villains* sixties concert, which I organised at Hammersmith last year, I'm trying to get BBC-TV to run a couple of specials devoted to sixties bands, though I don't know if this'll happen or not. Meanwhile I'm having some fun working with the band again and 1983 will see the release of the first DDDBM&T single to come out for several years. It's our version of Manfred Mann's ''Do Wah Diddy Diddy'' – our version being a lot heavier than the original. I think it's a fun thing, the sort of record that'll make people smile. We've had a great reaction whenever we've done it onstage and I just hope that record buyers feel the same way.'

The Karl Denver Trio

KARL DENVER HAD been around forever. He was around for years before the beat boom and he's still around now. But, partly due to the business acumen of producer Jack Good and partly due to public whim, Denver's trio became big, very big, during the first part of the sixties.

Delete that – change 'whim' for 'Wimoweh'. For that's the song by which Denver is best remembered, a high-voiced rendition of an African chant which Gordon Jenkins had arranged into an American hit some years earlier and which, during the eighties, was destined to become a hit yet again as 'The Lion Sleeps Tonight', a money-raker for Tight Fit. Not that 'Wimoweh' was Denver's first hit. Prior to that, he'd enjoyed Top Ten success with 'Marcheta' and 'Mexicali Rose', both songs which had delved into the then somewhat vague world of country-pop, during 1961.

Country boy Denver – really a Scot named Angus McKenzie, who preferred Tennessee to Tayside, had, as a teenager, joined the merchant navy and made his way around the world, eventually reaching Nashville, where he stayed for several years. Steeped in country music, he became so adept a practitioner that he even got a gig on *Grand Ole Opry*, Nashville's premier show, bringing his music not only to the ears of the American people but also to the notice of the immigration authorities who promptly booted him out of the country as an illegal immigrant. Jack Good, then the prime architect of most that was good in British pop, picked him up, produced his records and moulded him into something unique. And so it was that the Karl Denver Trio became oddball fixtures on the pop show circuit, their appeal lasting

reasonably well – through to the mid-sixties in fact. After which, the youthful portion of the group's record buyers suddenly decided that maybe the Trio's music wasn't hip after all.

Kevin Neill, the Trio's lead guitarist both then and now, recalls: 'We had some great times on those pop tours in the company of people like Billy Fury, Eden Kane, Joe Brown, Marty Wilde, Peter Jay and The Jaywalkers. Most of the others on those bills were in their teens, while we were already in our late twenties. In some ways they sort of looked up to us – though I don't think we led them the right way at times! But the funny thing was that we weren't really pop. We were essentially a country and western style cabaret act even then – Karl's always been pure country. Nevertheless, we did well and at one point had our own BBC2 series, *Side By Side*, on which we had The Beatles as our first guests.

'They came to us when we were playing a show up in Liverpool once and told us that they'd just made a record. Apparently they'd already tried to see Billy Fury but he wouldn't let them into his dressing room. Anyway, we liked what they did and had them on six of our shows. Also, we appeared on the American show *Shindig* with them. We've played with lots of people who have since made it. We worked with Little and Large back in 1959 at the Yew Tree, Manchester, the first pub that ever really put on entertainment. It was an amazing place holding around eight hundred people. Each show would attract coach-loads of people from all over the North. We made our best-ever album there – "With Love From Karl Denver". It was a great place to play.'

Since the mid-sixties, the cabaret dates and overseas tours have provided a steady income for the Denver Trio, one of the few outfits that maintained its original line-up right up to the eighties.

'I've been with Karl since the fifties, while our bass-player Jerry Cotterell only left two years ago, after a twenty-year stint, ill-health having forced him to quit. It was all the travelling that eventually got the better of him.' Constantly touring has not, apparently, ruined family life for either Neill or Denver, the former currently celebrating thirty years of happy marriage.

'Karl also is happily married. He's been married for about twelve years now, and has two boys, one ten years of age, the other four. It's his second marriage, the first lasted from 1954 up to the mid-sixties. And, yes, the constant touring can cause family problems for musicians, especially those who have married young. But it's surprising how many such marriages last considering the circumstances. Joe Brown, who always stays with us whenever he's in Manchester – all the band live in Manchester – his marriage has lasted well.'

Recent overseas tours have taken The Karl Denver Trio to such places as Australia and Zimbabwe – though one trip to Australia still causes Neill to suffer a mild attack of apoplexy every time he remembers it.

'We had a two-night stopover in Hong Kong, but when we tried to get back on the plane again, the customs people there asked us to pay fifteen hundred dollars because our equipment was adjudged to be excess weight. And we only had two hundred dollars on us! Luckily, the guy we talked to seemed to understand groups and he eventually let us through – though even then we had problems. The plane got to within a hundred miles of Manila and was then turned back. One way or another it took us four days to make that trip. At the same time Status Quo went over in style. They had two planes to themselves – one for the musicians and another just for their equipment!'

A favourite on the British country circuit, they played the Peterborough Country Music Festival in 1981 and again in 1983. And The Karl Denver Trio discovered, much to their delight, that at least one of their hits was a singalong favourite in Zimbabwe.

'When we worked over there it was a bit strange because Karl and I crack jokes and have a go at each other onstage. But in Zimbabwe we had to do everything through an interpreter. We'd do the jokes, he'd interpret them for the crowd and then the laughter would come, two or three seconds later. One thing though, we'd be doing these shows, mostly open-air concerts in front of about two thousand

people, and then we'd get to ''Wimoweh'', which, being an
African song, they all knew. And they'd all join in, banging
tin cans and everything. In some ways it was a bit eerie.'

Donovan

ONOVAN LEITCH really was the odd one out. Gentle, folksy, a genuine child of flower power, he turned up on *Ready, Steady, Go!* one night and charmed the nation with pure straight-off-the-street busker appeal. He wrote poems, sang protest songs, played wheezy harmonica and strummed a battered acoustic stickered 'this machine kills'. He looked kinda innocent and his voice had an oddball whine that somehow came out okay. Everybody tagged him as Scotland's answer to Bob Dylan and for a time, in Britain at least, he matched Hibbing's hero, hit for hit.

'Catch The Wind' was the first. It came out in early 1965 and Cathy McGowan thought it 'super'. Everybody else did too – with the result that it hung around the charts for some three months to be followed in turn by such other Donovan delights as 'Colours', 'Sunshine Superman', 'Mellow Yellow', 'There Is A Mountain', 'Jennifer Juniper' and 'Hurdy Gurdy Man'. Halfway through '69, he found an unlikely recording ally in ex-Yardbirds guitarist Jeff Beck and at producer Mickie Most's prompting, teamed up with Beck's group to cut 'Barabajagal', a big hit on both sides of the Atlantic. Then the seventies came in and Donovan went out. At least, that's the way it seemed on the surface. Halfway through the decade the *NME* ran an interview with him titled 'C'Mon You Guys, How'd You Get Into The Seventies' in which the Pied Piper – a role he'd played in Jacques Demy's 1971 film of that title – explained: 'It all seemed to peter out around 1969 or 1970. I didn't so much make a decision to stop touring, but went through a great kind of generation gap that affected a lot of people. I never felt like an entertainer. I wanted to keep my relation with peace, freedom, dreams and fairytales. And it came about that there was no real excitement.'

Not that Donovan ever became a real loser. He initially took an enforced sabbatical while business and financial problems were sorted out, did the odd concert or two, worked on the score for Zeffirelli's *Brother Sun, Sister Moon* movie, and then signed a lucrative contract with Epic Records. In October, 1970, he caught up with and married Linda Lawrence, whom he'd initially met on *Ready, Steady, Go!* in 1965, shortly after she'd broken up with Brian Jones, the father of her son Julian. Donovan had immediately fallen for her, and penned 'Sunshine Superman' in her honour. And then he'd gone through a period of pain and uncertainty as Linda headed out for LA, where she remained for the next five years, leaving Don career-climbing in Europe. Well, at least the seventies put that one right.

Donovan, who at one point zoomed around in an Aston Martin and lived in a mansion near Elton John's place, opted for the simple life once more and eventually found somewhere to call home near Joshua Tree, California, way out in the desert, where he lived in what he termed 'humble' fashion. His deal with Epic guaranteed him twenty thousand dollars a year for five years. In return he turned out a series of albums for the label – including a Nashville-recorded job named with somewhat wry humour '7-Tease', and then watched them fizzle into obscurity as he failed to supply the usual back-up tours. Sure, Don wasn't above doing the odd concert or two but, encouraged by Linda, he didn't push things too far and didn't really come out of hiding until 1976.

Interviewed then, he claimed that though he lived in quiet manner, he still had managed to hold on to his wealth by investing in property – his ownership at that point extending to three small Skye islands, a sixteenth-century cottage in a Hertfordshire wood, where his wife's parents lived, plus a monastery set amid thirty acres of country in County Galway. It was also in '76 that he started touring extensively once more, initially working with a band called Jiva, while in '77 he played some ninety dates including a number in Britain.

That year he renewed his acquaintance with Mickie Most once more, Most being the producer who had helped him gain the majority of his biggest successes. He cut an album for Most's RAK label but it seemed that the Donovan era was well and truly over and the disc failed to sell, as did 'Dare To Be Different', a 1978 single.

It was nearly three years before he made another real attempt to re-establish himself as a major figure in the world of music. After playing a much-hailed set at the 1981 Cambridge Folk Festival, he played an October concert at London's Festival Hall and announced that he was back on the recording scene once more.

Around that time too, he settled down in Britain again. He and Linda, plus Julian, now in his twenties, and Don's two daughters, Astella and Oriole, began living in a large Victorian house, not an archer's shot from the turrets of Windsor Castle.

And, despite the realisation that he is now unlikely to ever achieve the kind of success that made him a headline name at the age of nineteen, he's far from unhappy.

'I lived to free myself from my beginnings,' he told the *Sunday Express*'s Lynn Barber in 1982. 'I lived to rise above society and speak to it. I have done that, which is the real success. So I have no regrets.'

Craig Douglas

LOOKING BACK, IT'S hard to believe that he really was a star. His looks were nothing startling and his voice likewise. He didn't seem to possess much in the way of charisma or, for that matter, anything else that teen heroes needed to get hordes of autograph hunters lining up at the stage door. But a star Craig Douglas undoubtedly was. With nine Top Twenty hits and a number of film appearances to prove the point. Not at all bad for an ex-milkman from the Isle of Wight.

At the time of pint-pushing he was plain Terence Perkins, one of ten children born in Newport on the Isle of Wight. He won a fiver in a local talent contest and changed his name after being discovered amid a Jack Good *Six-Five Special* TV show. More importantly, he gained a shrewd manager in Bunny Lewis and, from then on, made all the right moves and the right connections. The result was two hit records in 1959 – the first a wimpy version of 'A Teenager In Love' followed by an even wimpier cover of Sam Cooke's 'Only Sixteen'. As the sixties moved in, Douglas rivalled Cliff Richard as king-pin on the British pop scene, showing remarkable consistency as a chart climber. In 1960, he came up with 'Pretty Blue Eyes' and 'The Heart Of A Teenage Girl'. During '61, he kept up the momentum with 'A Hundred Pounds Of Clay' and 'Time', while 1962 brought even more kudos with the release of 'When My Little Girl Is Smiling', 'Our Favourite Melodies' and 'Oh, Lonesome Me'.

It mattered little that most of these songs were available in superior versions by other artists; Douglas, bless his brylcreemed quiff, was the man in charge. It was in '62 that he also gained his first starring film role, teaming up with Helen Shapiro in *It's Trad Dad*, a cheapo movie whose only importance, these days, is that it was the first pop involvement of director Dick Lester, who later made The Beatles' *A Hard Day's Night* and *Help!* classics. Nevertheless, at the time, it was an important step for Douglas to make.

'I feel that filming is much more demanding and exacting than many people believe and so I am keen to serve a full apprenticeship before doing anything that saps my acting ability,' claimed Douglas, commenting on the slight role the film provided. As good as his word, while doing summer shows at Hastings and Weston-super-Mare that year, he began learning something about stagecraft from actress Beryl Reid. 'I've thought about taking a strong, dramatic role, one with no singing, if only someone would offer it to me,' said Douglas, realising that he couldn't remain a teen dream forever. And he couldn't. He had a single called 'Town Crier', which came out in early '63 and just scraped into the Top Forty. It was then that the beat groups muscled in on his territory and the demand for boy-next-door popsters disappeared somewhere up the Mersey tunnel.

If nothing else, Craig Douglas proved adaptable. He moved into show-biz proper, the world of cabaret, musical-comedy and panto. By the seventies he was established on the Caesar's Palace, Room At The Top, Quaglino's circuit, gaining notices that commented on his 'easy sophistication and easy manner', his 'charm and romantic style', rated 'perfect for a dining and dancing audience' etc. Utilising special material, penned for him by the ever-caring Bunny Lewis, and with the hangovers from his teenage past spiced with a flurry of show songs, Douglas turned increasingly to the swish hotel market, playing the Intercontinental, in Nairobi, the Carlton, in Jo'burg, inevitably returning to Britain once a year to appear in *Cinderella* or *Babes In The Wood*. And if his Brel interpretations failed to garner the sort of attention once claimed by such as Scott Walker, he at least never ducked out, never threw a moody and kept on keeping on.

Surprisingly, Craig Douglas never did move into the world

of acting. There have been no films since *It's Trad Dad* and his stage appearances have been limited to revivals of shows such as *No, No, Nanette* and *Lock Up Your Daughters*, his only dramatic role coming in a version of the well-known thriller *Wait Until Dark*. For him it's been a story of unending encounters with the supper-club set, cloth cap nights at working men's clubs and romantic duets with fairy-tale princesses amid hardboard castles. Today, as his management's handout informs you: 'Craig is unmarried, lives in a flat in Knightsbridge, has a golf handicap of nine, rides, plays tennis, table tennis, snooker and also indulges in backgammon. He has never had a nervous breakdown or freaked out and, in a sense, has at times suffered for his clean image.'

He still does all right too. When I phoned the Lewis-Joelle company in order to talk to him, I was informed: 'Craig's playing a season in Malta right now.' I mean, that can't be bad. Can it?

The Equals in 1983

The Equals

THERE'S A POPULAR fallacy that Eddy Grant was once lead vocalist with The Equals. Early in 1983, when Grant was hit-parading with 'Electric Avenue', one daily paper even ran a competition in which readers were asked to name the sixties band for whom he provided the lead vocals. Snag was, if the expected answer – The Equals – was provided, it would have been the wrong one. Though, it seems, not even the paper knew that. Derv Gordon did, though.

For Derv was – and still is – The Equals' frontman. He and his twin brother Lincoln, born Kingston, Jamaica, were brought up in North London, where they teamed with Guyanan Grant and some other school mates to form a multiracial band in 1966. And as many of the beat group boomsters faded from the scene, the band, called The Equals and featuring a line-up comprising Derv (vocals), Lincoln Gordon (rhythm guitar), Eddy Grant (lead guitar), Pat Lloyd (guitar) and John Hall (drums), made their bubblegum bid for fame. They signed to a minor label, President, and their chances of making an impact didn't seem all that hot at first. But they did fairly well with a single called 'I Get So Excited' in early '68 and their next one, 'Baby Come Back', proved a veritable monster, climbing all over the charts and leaving the way open for a number of other hits – among the most potent being 'Laurel And Hardy', 'Viva Bobby Joe' and 'Black Skin Boys', the last-named providing the band with a stepping stone into the seventies. Then, with eight chart successes to their name in under three years, The Equals ceased making records. So what happened?

A news item in *Record Retailer*, dated June 1973, provided the answer. It read: 'The two year dispute between The Equals and the President label has been settled out of court. The group has also signed a new three-year contract with President and recording sessions started this week at Regent Sound for a new double-album and single. Singer and guitarist Eddie Grant (Grant always spelt his name with an "ie" in those days) is to be associated with the group again in a production and songwriting capacity, though he has no plans to make any personal appearances with the band.'

Grant, the son of a trumpet-playing father, had, in the meantime, put in a little time as an actor (no duffer; along the way he's appeared at the Royal Court Theatre and also turned up in the Beeb's *Onedin Line* TV series), challenged Enoch Powell to a debate and put together Coach House Studios, the first black-owned recording studio in Europe. In 1974, he formed his own company, Ice Records, registered in his native Guyana, and began producing records not only for The Equals – who had relinquished their ties with President – but also for such acts as The Pioneers, The Mexicano, Lord Kitchener and 90 Inclusive. In 1977, as The Equals split up, Eddy Grant became a business supremo, starting an Ice Records office in the UK and also moving into Nigeria and Canada. His success in these territories proved enormous – in 1979 he became the first artist in the history of EMI-Nigeria to receive three gold discs for three albums released in a single year. That same year, with Ice linked with the Ensign label in Britain, he put out a reggae-cum-disco single called 'Living On The Front Line' and gained his first UK solo hit. Since that time Grant, who now lives with his wife and family in a colonial plantation house in Barbados, has bombarded the charts with such hits as 'Do You Feel My Love?', 'Can't Get Enough Of You', 'I Love You, Yes I Love You', 'I Don't Wanna Dance' and 'Electric Avenue'. Not surprisingly, he's an extremely wealthy man and, recordwise, one of the hottest properties in the world outside of the USA, which he's certain he will conquer in due course. Certainly, he can seemingly sell records anywhere. Even in 1982, with Britain and the Argentine engaged in war over the Falklands, he had two

singles in the Argentinian Top Five at the same time, along
with that country's biggest selling album. A non-smoker,
non-drinker and a vehement anti-drug man, Grant has few
vices. The Equals one-time songwriter and Mr Fix-It is
justifiably proud of what he has achieved since the first day
that the band first stepped into a studio. 'On that day,' he'll
tell you, 'I said to Mr Edward Kassner, who was boss of
President Records – Look, you now have Kassner House.
One day I'm gonna have Grant House, this is just my
apprenticeship.'

The career of his fellow Equals is now currently picking up
again after a few lean years which one or two members of the
band spent on the dole. Pat Lloyd, who acts as their
spokesman these days, admits that things haven't been that
great for them since '77.

'We toured the Caribbean around 1975 playing Guyana
and Barbados – Eddy played as part of the band during that
trip – and then we returned home to make an album for
Phonogram which was very much like the sort of thing that
Eddy's doing now. A single called "Funky Like A Train"
came from those sessions but it didn't do anything. Soon
after, we broke up. I still had an income from Grant Music, a
company that Eddy and I own jointly. I continued to help run
the company and did some writing and production work.
Lincoln – he played with a reggae band for a while but did
nothing spectacular, while Derv – well, let's just say that he
was the one who saved all his money.

'We kept in contact until just over a year ago, when a
German promoter offered us a tour if we would get back
together again. At first we said "why?", then we said: "why
not?" After all, the money offered was really too good to
refuse. So we rehearsed for six weeks and went over and
played the dates. Since then we've been back for one-offs here
and there and we've got another big tour lined up for 1983.
We were always very big in Germany; we had thirteen Top
Twenty hits there and it was always a lot different to playing
in Britain. Here it's always been something of a funny
situation because we weren't really a sixties band. We came
up right at the end of the decade and don't fit in with bands

like The Searchers and all those other outfits who are part of the revival scenes. It's true that we had hits like "Baby Come Back" but that wasn't all that The Equals were about. People forget that when we did "Black Skin Blue Eyed Boys", some radio people wouldn't even play it because it wasn't the sort of thing they expected from us. I suppose in some ways we've always been a little bit too far ahead. But right now we're back in the studios again making a new album, which Hal Carter is producing. We've replaced Eddy with a keyboard player named John Jago and our current sound is a lot different from that which people associate with the original band. We're still very aggressive though – which we always were. Maybe if things work out we won't have to face thirty-five or thirty-six-year-old fans pinning us against the wall and asking us to do "Baby Come Back" yet again. That would be some sort of relief.'

Marianne Faithfull

MARIANNE FAITHFULL MUST have been an inspiration to every dolly bird of the mid-sixties. She couldn't sing to save her life. But she looked great – both unimaginably sexy and unbelievably innocent – and when she smiled sadly, the effect was so memorable that most males perceiving her on *Ready, Steady, Go!* would immediately dash off to the nearest record shop and buy several copies of her latest release. She had class too. The daughter of a countess, no less. Married to art student John Dunbar while still at school, she got to know all the right people, got invited to all the right parties. And though she was the mother of Dunbar's child, no one was really surprised when she elected to jet off with Mick Jagger, thereafter providing enough copy to keep the popular press happy for yonks.

At the time she made her first recording, a shaky version of Jagger and Richard's 'As Tears Go By', she was still at convent school, in Reading. To promote the disc, she did live and TV shows during her school holidays. Then, realising that, despite her lack of voice, she could sell records on image alone, she opted for a full-time career in pop, enjoying three further major successes in 1965 with 'Come And Stay With Me', 'This Little Bird' and 'Summer Nights'. When the hits stopped coming, the stories continued. Gleefully, the press reported how she was caught in a state of semi-nudity during one police raid. True, she upped her respectability rating by playing in a Chekhov play at the Royal Court, but next moment though she was reverting to type and accepting roles in films like *Girl On A Motorcycle* in which she, naked under her leathers, was called upon to rush into her screen lover's

bedroom pleading with him to 'skin her'. In real life she rushed just as haphazardly from one situation to another. In 1968 it was announced that she was pregnant by Jagger, though no marriage was in sight. Then came a miscarriage, followed by a period of deep depression. Soon she was into heroin.

In Australia, waiting for Mick Jagger to finish filming *Ned Kelly*, in 1969, she made the first of her suicide bids. A year later, faced with Marianne's total reliance on drugs and the knowledge that his own career was likely to be jeopardised by a drug squad raid at any time, Jagger headed out of her life and into the arms of Bianca Perez Moreno de Marias.

With Mick gone and an affair with Italian film director Mario Shifano also relegated to the past, Marianne resumed her acting career, playing Ophelia opposite Nicol Williamson's Hamlet in Tony Richardson's film and also gaining parts in a number of plays. Not for long the smooth path, however. Soon she was reported as being hospitalised for a 'rest' after being found ill in a Birmingham hotel bedroom. And, sometime after this, she was discovered stoned and tottering down a London street. The first of her attempts to kick her drug addiction followed, though by 1973 she had registered at Bexley Hospital in an effort to obtain her drugs on the National Health scheme. 'I was paying a pound a jack and couldn't afford it,' she told *Rolling Stone* magazine, also revealing at the same time that she'd been sacked from an Edinburgh stage show because of her addiction and that Bell Records had rejected an album she had made.

At the age of twenty-six she made something of a comeback. Following a period of seventeen months without drugs — 'It was painful — but then, I get very determined' — she grabbed a part in a John Osborne play. And a couple of years later, she bounced back on the music scene once more, working with a band headed by guitarist Bev Brierley, whom she has since married, and going out on the road. An album with NEMS Records also surfaced around this time. Titled 'Dreamin' My Dreams', it topped the Irish charts but elsewhere remained something of an unofficial secret.

By 1979, virtually written off as a singer, Marianne made another stab at recording. Signing with Island Records she attempted a bitter, bruising album which was well-received by the critics called 'Broken English' and though it ran into immediate problems – the record contained an overly explicit love song in 'Why D'Ya Do It?', resulting in an EMI distribution ban – the breakthrough was made. Amazingly, there was even a mild hit single with 'The Ballad Of Lucy Jordan', Marianne's first chart disc for over thirteen years.

These days she resides in a modest London abode with Bev Brierley, while teenage son Nicholas lives with his father, John Dunbar. She's logged yet another outstanding album in 'Dangerous Acquaintances' plus a not-so-hot one in 'A Child's Adventure' and though she's sometimes worried by attacks of laryngitis, which occur whenever she's tired or overworked, Marianne Faithfull remains as defiant as ever. She abhors the sixties survivor tag and recently told *Goldmine*'s Marianne Meyer: 'I hate the word "survivor". I like the word "winner". To survive is not enough, you have to do more than that. I want to have a daughter. I want to write novels. I'm not going to sacrifice myself on this altar of rock and roll.'

The Fourmost

A GLANCE THROUGH back editions of *Merseybeat* shows that in January, 1962, The Blue Jays were the tenth most popular band in Liverpool. Discovering that there was already a Scottish group of that name, they switched to become The Four Mosts, a handle that remained until Brian Epstein became their manager and decided that the title The Fourmost would look better on the billboards.

Originally their line-up was Brian O'Hara (lead guitar), Joey Bower (rhythm guitar), Billy Hatton (bass) and Dave Lovelady (drums), Bower being replaced by Mike Millward when the group went fully professional. The Epstein connection meant that they were offered a couple of Lennon-McCartney songs for their first two singles, something roughly akin to being given a licence to print money in 1963–64. So 'Hello Little Girl' and 'I'm In Love' both went Top Twenty quick as a flash and nobody, but nobody, was in the least surprised. 'Lennon and McCartney, innit?' said the knowing ones – and The Fourmost decided that it was time for a switch.

Next time around they recorded a song penned by Russ Alquist, Juliet Mills' husband. Titled 'A Little Loving' it charted even higher than the two Beatle compositions. It seemed that everything was going the band's way.

Onstage they'd developed into quite a comedy act. They did an eight-month spell at the London Palladium in 1964 and captivated family audiences. They also continued pleasing the kids and were asked to appear on various Beatle shows, in 1965 being signed to appear in the Merseybeat movie, *Ferry Cross The Mersey*. But their luck had begun to run out. Mike

Millward had become seriously ill and was forced to leave them for a while. He returned after some months and struggled on, despite declining health, due to leukaemia, till his death in 1966. Billy Hatton later told of Millward's struggle in Spencer Leigh's book *Stars In My Eyes*.

'Mike left the group for four months to have some radium treatment for a growth in his throat. He came back and we watched him slowly decline. He didn't want to leave the group. We were at the Palladium and his hair would be falling out in huge clumps. We'd put it back again with Sellotape before we went on stage. Eventually though, the blood drained away and he died.'

Then in 1967, Brian Epstein also died. Not much seemed to be going right for the band. Even their records weren't selling any more.

But with Joey Bower back to replace Millward, The Fourmost carried on. They still had a recording contract and The Beatles remained their friends. Indeed, Paul McCartney made a vain attempt to brighten up The Fourmost's waning record career by producing 'Rosetta', a 1969 single, for the group.

Realising that they'd outgrown their teen appeal, The Fourmost settled down to life on the cabaret circuit during the seventies, slotting in a large number of overseas dates along the way. And so things continued, almost into the eighties: Bower, Hatton, Lovelady and O'Hara stuck together till, realising they were on an ever-downhill trail, the first three quit, Bower and Lovelady investing in a decorating business while Hatton got involved with a garage.

Brian O'Hara promptly got together with an existing band in order to keep The Fourmost name available for club bookings and later completely revamped the group. At the tail-end of 1979, a group called Clouds could be found working at various Liverpool nighteries. It comprised Dave Lovelady, Billy Hatton, Joey Bower and Bower's wife Lesley. And so the music-making continued. Brian O'Hara finally quit The Fourmost in February, 1982 leaving the band in the hands of John Campbell, who was at that time drummer with the outfit. Campbell, who has also since become the band's manager, explains:

'Brian, who'd increasingly gotten into comedy and had his own comedy spot in the show, decided he'd had enough of The Fourmost. He's currently running a garage and selling secondhand cars. Incidentally, Billy Hatton also runs a separate business from the same garage. In the meantime, I've kept The Fourmost going with the aid of bassist Billy Haisman, who also handles most of the lead vocals, and two guitarists – Ronnie Hughes, who's actually Billy Haisman's brother, and Bernie Crossley. Apart from playing drums I also do the Frankie Valli-type vocals. Everybody in the band comes from Liverpool – The Fourmost has always been a Liverpool band and I intend to keep it that way – and the main change that has been made is that we've dropped all the comedy and got back to music. Which is how things started out, right back at the beginning. These days we do lots of four-part vocal harmony things with twin guitar backings. The material is mainly sixties stuff – The Beach Boys, Four Seasons etc – along with the original Fourmost stuff, of course. And in the main we work the cabaret circuit, along with the odd other thing or two, like appearing on the *Unforgettable* TV show at the end of '82.'

The Four Pennies

IT WASN'T UNTIL I bumped into Fritz Fryer, at Monmouth's Rockfield Studios during one mid-seventies recording session, that I remembered The Four Pennies. Fryer had been bass-player with the Blackburn-based quartet back in the days when they'd been The Lionel Morton Four. Lead singer Morton had been a choir member at Blackburn Cathedral for some seven years. But it was as The Four Pennies – Morton and Fryer teaming with Mike Wilsh (guitar and piano) and Alan Buck (drums) – that the break-through came. They signed a recording contract with Philips and made a Merseybeatish single called 'Do You Want Me To' which made a very minor dent in the chart at the start of '64. Next they switched direction and cut a well-rounded ballad called 'Juliet' penned by Morton himself. Released in April, 1964, it gradually climbed the listings till it reached Number One, toppling The Searchers' 'Don't Throw Your Love Away' and fighting off a challenge from Millie's 'My Boy Lollipop'. Both Morton and Fryer had good voices and all that was required to keep the band going was a supply of strong material. But there was never enough. There were two more hits in '64 – 'I Found Out The Hard Way' and 'Black Girl' – plus a Top Twenty shot with 'Until It's Time For You To Go' in 1965, after which The Four Pennies became devalued as a chart act, only 'Trouble Is My Middle Name', a mild success in 1966, providing the quartet with any cause for hope.

Alan Buck, now a freelance professional manager in the music biz, remembers: 'We did our last dates in Istanbul, around February-March, 1967. Maybe if we could have

obtained one more really big hit we'd have stuck together. But we were starved of good material. We needed a lot more of that. Lionel was married to Julia Foster, who'd been in several films (*Alfie*, *Half A Sixpence* etc) and was doing well in the West End – and he wanted to go solo, maybe to keep up with his wife's achievements. When Lionel went, that was it. We tried one or two other singers after that Turkish trip but with that band you couldn't alter the front line. Without either Lionel or Fritz we wouldn't have what it needed to get to Number One. We could have carried on in cabaret, I suppose, but we didn't want to do that forever.'

So the foursome went their various ways, Fryer initially forming an outfit known as Fritz, Mike and Mo before becoming a highly regarded producer, working with such acts as Horslips, Stackridge, Motorhead, Clannad, Squeeze and Prelude, masterminding the latter's 'After The Goldrush' hit single. Later, he tired of the music scene and moved to the Ross-on-Wye area where he currently runs a flourishing business in antique lighting.

Alan Buck became producer at Radio Luxembourg for a time. His other positions during the seventies and early eighties included that of professional manager at Sunbury Music and UA Music, label manager at Bell Records, A&R co-ordinator at Phonogram and professional manager at Burlington Music.

'I still really miss playing,' he says. 'In fact Lionel, Mike Wilsh and I nearly got together a short while ago. There's a lot of work in North Wales on the cabaret and club scene and Lionel, who's now re-married, thought he'd put a band together to play on that circuit. But he didn't want to do the old act – it was all new stuff. I wasn't interested because I felt it wouldn't mean anything. The kind of material they were doing was a bit like a constipated Edmundo Ros and all a bit pointless. Certainly I wasn't going to mess around on congas and all that sort of thing. Maybe if we could have got the old act back together things could work. Then again, if Fritz wasn't included those vocals wouldn't be quite right. And those vocals were the main thing. We were a vocal band really. Fritz still sings, y'know. Takes his guitar into pubs and does solo things. He's got a great voice now, better than ever. We went into a studio during 1980 to try out a couple of songs and his voice seems to have quadrupled in strength since our Four Pennies days. It's really quite amazing!'

Freddie And The Dreamers

I TUNED INTO Channel Four's *Unforgettable* show one night in late '82 and there was Freddie Garrity, still leading a version of The Dreamers, still doing his dotty dances and, inevitably, yelling 'justaminit' as he cavorted through re-runs of 'If You Gotta Make A Fool Of Somebody' and 'I'm Telling You Now', generally engaging in personifying the term 'perpetual motion'. Once a Manchester milkman who generally finished his round late because he was always gagging with customers, Garrity worked in skiffle groups and local bands before forming Freddie and The Dreamers during 1959. A showman after Barnum's own heart, he moved into the beat group era with considerable vigour. A cross between Buddy Holly and Harold Lloyd, he sang and performed in zany manner, often doing the splits in mid-air and singing in a high-pitched voice that suggested he'd sat down on something nasty.

He was fun and everybody loved him, the mums and dads, the big kids and the even bigger kids. Especially in 1963. For that was when he had three Top Five records with 'If You Gotta Make A Fool Of Somebody', 'I'm Telling You Now' and 'You Were Made For Me'. Not bad going, even by Beatle standards.

Next year things fell off a little and only 'I Understand' went Top Five – though 'Over You' and 'I Love You Baby' both climbed into the Top Twenty.

Garrity had got his dream bungalow and a Jag to put in the garage. And he hadn't finished yet. For while The Dreamers' hits petered out in Britain during 1965, Freddie's conquest of American had begun. And it became instantly apparent that American mums, dads and their variously sized offspring

WILLIAMS
DEACON'S
BANK

loved Garrity's eccentricities as much as their British counterparts. As a result 'I'm Telling You Now' went to the top of the American charts, selling a zillion copies.

It wasn't only the half-pint Mancunian's singing that turned them all on. They went absolutely potty about his dancing too. 'What's that dance called?' they asked, conscious of their own Black Bottom, Charleston, Twist and Hully Gully heritage.

Garrity thought for a moment and then replied: 'It's called The Freddie', promptly recording a number of that very title, which rocketed into the Top Twenty.

Being such a visual act, Garrity and his men were certs for the movies. After doing the usual guest spots on such shebangs as *What A Crazy World*, *Just For Fun* and *Everyday's A Holiday*, they were booked to play the leading roles – as a group of dim-witted boy scouts! – in the 1965 film *Cuckoo Patrol*.

'Juvenile humour!' proclaimed the pundits. But that's what Freddie Garrity was all about. Sometimes it seemed that the most enterprising thing he did was to leap in the air and drop his trousers. Woody Allen he wasn't. When the novelty of Garrity's approach wore off, so the hits petered out. And then he turned increasingly to an obvious market – children's entertainment, pantomime and suchlike.

At the end of the sixties, he gave up full-time touring with his band and together with the Dreamers' bassist Pete Birrell, turned to children's TV for much of his work, the twosome becoming regulars on the long-running kids' show *Little Big Time*.

By 1975 Garrity claimed to be spending ten weeks each year in pantomime, sixteen weeks in summer season, thirteen weeks on children's TV and six weeks in cabaret, taking the rest of the time in holiday.

'I'm still making the same amount of money as I was ten years ago,' he told one journalist. 'In fact, more now because I'm on my own.'

And in 1983 he was still able to boast: 'Over the last twenty years, since we first went into the charts, I think we've only had a couple of weeks without work when we wanted it – and that was due to a mix-up in bookings!'

Billy Fury on his farm

Billy Fury

IT'S BEEN SAID that Billy Fury was the only truly great British rock'n'roll star. And in the late fifties, when he formed part of promoter Larry Parnes' pop circus – along with Marty Wilde, Tommy Steele, Dickie Pride, Duffy Power, Vince Eager and a legion of other names – he was easily the greasiest, sexiest, most angst-ridden heart-throb of them all.

Originally he'd been just plain Ronald Wycherly from the Dingle, Liverpool. A tearaway, he'd already got the push from a couple of jobs because of his penchant for punch-ups. But he bummed around, sang whenever anyone would pay him to do so and, eventually, got bundled onstage at the Birkenhead Essoldo to play a set at short notice, where his act sent all attending Scousers into something approaching frenzy.

Signed by Parnes, he got a record deal with Decca and had a major hit with 'Maybe Tomorrow', his very first record, in 1959, claiming his initial Top Ten entry with 'Colette' during the following year.

For the next five years there was no holding him. He played sell-out tours all over the place, got banned in Ireland for being obscene onstage, starred in films, appeared on just about every worthwhile pop radio and TV show and continually went Top Ten with records like 'Halfway To Paradise', 'Jealousy', 'I'll Never Find Another You', 'Last Night Was Made For Love', 'Once Upon A Dream', 'Like I've Never Been Gone', 'When Will I Say I Love You', 'In Summer' and 'In Thoughts Of You', though, surprisingly, he never had a Number One.

It was midway through the sixties that the hits ran out, forcing Fury to quit playing to the kids and to move into cabaret. Parnes was still his agent and continued to find him all the best, most lucrative jobs. But Fury had a history of childhood and teenage illness that had caused him to spend lengthy periods of time in the confines of various hospitals; rheumatic fever left him with a damaged heart, a condition which eventually caught up with him in 1967.

'One of the valves in my heart had closed up,' Fury remembered, 'And the blood wasn't getting through. The only way for the blood to come out was through my mouth. That was one of the very bad symptoms that I had. So I had to quit.' Offstage, Fury had been, and remained, an introvert who preferred animals to people, a situation reflected in the 1965 film *I've Gotta Horse*, in which he portrayed a pop star who loved a racehorse even more than his career. So, for a while, he dropped out of music and retired to a farm in Sussex, remaining there until 1970, when heart surgeons were able to perform an operation that brought renewed good health for a period.

It was around this time that Fury became bored with the orderly nature of the English countryside and decided to move where things were more rugged. He bought a sheep-farm near Llandovery, in the Welsh mountains, and there devoted most of his attention to such activities as lambing and sheep-shearing, keeping his bank balance straight by playing the odd live date or two, or maybe appearing on a rock'n'roll nostalgia tour, as he did in the company of Marty Wilde, Carl Simmons, Heinz, The Tornados and Tommy Bruce, during 1974.

Films still beckoned – Fury appeared as rocker Stormy Tempest in *That'll Be The Day*, emotively handling such songs as Pete Townshend's 'Long Live Rock' and Viv Stanshall's 'What In The World' – and even the odd record or two materialised, though all this activity came to an end in 1975, when the singer's health once more failed him and a second heart operation had to be performed.

For a while, he kept his onstage appearances down to a minimum, playing a few cabaret and club dates but mainly spending time with his sheep and horses, also taking care of any wild life that the local RSPCA saw fit to leave in his charge, and also, when in more militant mood, indulging in a flurry of anti-blood sport protests.

In the autumn of 1982, despite the knowledge that any undue exertions could end his life, Billy Fury began planning a new album, a comeback tour and radio and TV appearances. 'I need the warmth of an audience,' he claimed, as he taped an *Unforgettable* session for transmission on Channel Four. Then he started out on his series of shows with Pepsi And The Colas, his young back-up band, and began recording for his Polydor album. On Thursday, January 27, Fury worked late into the night at the studio, then returned to his London address, at Cavendish Avenue, St John's Wood, where he was staying with his girl friend of ten years, Lisa Rosen. There he experienced a heart attack and was rushed to hospital. But it was too late. At just after midday on January 28, he was pronounced dead. And, even though he'd not had a real hit for over fifteen years, Fury's death grabbed the headlines in all the papers and dominated the radio and TV newscasts. His funeral, a few days later, again attracted a considerable amount of media coverage, the mourners including Jess Conrad, Eden Kane, Larry Parnes, and Marty Wilde, the singer who had encouraged Fury to make that all-important appearance at the Birkenhead Essoldo back in '59.

Fury's father, Albert Wycherly, a retired British Airways steward, later said: 'We went to London last month to see him and he seemed in fine spirits. He thought he was on the verge of a big comeback after a lot of years of ill health and he was very excited about the prospects.'

Not that Fury himself had any illusions. He knew that he might be setting out on his last fling. Rumour had it that he had even helped compile a memorial album that would be released in the event of his death. Nevertheless, he was determined not to go out on a losing streak. And he didn't – for, only a few days after his death, his 'Hit Parade' compilation began climbing the charts, to be followed in turn by 'The Only One', an album formed from the tracks Fury completed during his final days.

'He was the greatest performing artist that the UK has ever seen,' Larry Parnes stated on hearing of Fury's death. A lot of people agreed with him.

Gerry And The Pacemakers

GERRY AND THE PACEMAKERS, the second band to be signed by Brian Epstein, actually beat The Beatles to the punch, becoming the first of the Liverpool groups to top the UK charts. They also had the distinction of being the only act to log Number Ones with their first three releases – 'How Do You Do It?', 'I Like It' and 'You'll Never Walk Alone' – the first two also going Top Twenty on the other side of the Atlantic.

Originally there'd been The Mars Bars, formed by vocalist-guitarist Gerry Marsden and his brother Freddie, who thrashed about on drums. Teaming up with bassist Les Chadwick, they became The Pacemakers and in the early sixties, like umpteen other Scouse outfits, they made the trip to Hamburg, playing the Top Ten Club in that city. After adding pianist Les McGuire, they became part of the Epstein empire and were quickly provided with a brace of 1963 hits by tunesmith Mitch Murray. Their third hit, a song from Rodgers and Hammerstein's *Carousel*, is remembered in Liverpool to this day. For their version of 'You'll Never Walk Alone' not only resulted in a single that clung to a place in the charts for nineteen weeks, but also supplied Anfield with a soccer anthem that'll probably be sung as long as kids wave red scarves on The Kop.

Though '63 proved a momentous year for Marsden and his mates, 1964 was even better, thanks to a number of American hits, and further British winners: 'I'm The One', 'Don't Let The Sun Catch You Crying' and 'Ferry Cross The Mersey', which was the title song from a feature film that provided The Pacemakers with starring roles.

GRETS

Then, almost as quickly as things had got under way, the band's career came to a halt. Well, not quite that quickly. They did have one Top Twenty single in Britain during 1965 with 'I'll Be There'. And in America, where things were running about a year behind, music-wise, they accrued not-to-be-sneered-at sales with a single called 'Girl On A Swing', in the autumn of 1966.

Later that same year, Gerry and the original Pacemakers parted company without much ado. 'We'd been travelling around for five or six years,' explained Gerry Marsden, 'and we decided to just pack it in. I wanted to do cabaret and also get into the West End, because that had always been an ambition of mine.' During '67 he began cutting solo discs for CBS without much success but had more luck in the European Song Cup contest at Knokke-Le-Zoutte, Belgium, where he led the British team to victory. He was also involved as compere on a *Disney In Wonderland* TV show and, in 1968, achieved his ambition by appearing as Joe Studholme in the London West End presentation of *Charlie Girl*, a long-running musical that kept Marsden gainfully employed for about two-and-a-half years.

From there, things plummeted a little. Like Freddie Garrity, he became a children's entertainer for four years, his main stint being on TV's *The Sooty Show*, where he played straight man to Harry Corbett's puppets. During that time, however, there was something of a renewal of interest in Merseybeat in the USA and Gerry put together a new version of The Pacemakers to play a Richard Nader-produced concert at New York's Madison Square Garden in 1973. Not long after, he signed yet another recording contract – this time with DJM – and, along with making some solo items, also came up with the first new Gerry And The Pacemakers single for several years.

Not that it mattered. The new records sold about as well as bow-ties in Bootle. Nevertheless, bookings for the band rolled in steadily and in 1975 The Pacemakers found themselves embarking on a two-month tour of Australia, since which time, Marsden and the band – the subject of frequent personnel changes in recent years – have continued notching up the odd tour or two overseas, while further enhancing their reputation as a good draw on the home chicken-in-a-basket circuit. So, while nobody's bothered to cut any new Gerry Marsden recordings between 1974 and 1983, when he signed to the Deb label, he's never been short of work and – unlike several other sixties heroes – his face remains unknown at the job centre.

In 1982 he played to one of the biggest audiences he'd faced in recent years when he attended Liverpool Cathedral for the funeral service of Liverpool FC's much-beloved ex-manager Bill Shankly. There, for old times' sake, he reprised 'You'll Never Walk Alone' and the tears simply streamed down the cheeks of even the most hard-bitten Scousers. It's doubtful if the Marsden voice has ever been received in such an emotional manner.

Today he's still Gerry Marsden, the ordinary-looking, likeable sort who once happened to be in the right place at the right time and had the good sense to make the most of things while they were going. Around the time of the DJM recording dates it was suggested to him that he might have achieved more during the seventies and eighties if, like such other early sixties rockers as Shane Fenton (who became Alvin Stardust) and Paul Raven (who became Gary Glitter), he'd maybe changed his name or opted for another image. But Gerry merely shook his head and replied: 'I think that sort of show-biz is great but it's not for me. I'm too small and ugly to be a sex-symbol. I can only be myself – If I was in a glitter suit or leathers, I'd just collapse laughing half-way through the first song!'

Jet Harris

WHENEVER THE SUBJECT of rock'n'roll losers is invoked, the name of Jet Harris inevitably crops up early in the conversation. He had everything going for him – looks, image, ability . . . the whole caboodle. Yet, just a few months after being voted Britain's most outstanding pop instrumentalist, his career was in tatters. Hello and goodbye. That was Jet Harris.

Back in the days when he could only afford half pints, he was Terry Harris, a bass-player from Wembley. Together with his mate, Tony Meehan, he became part of two very successful groups, The Vipers and The Shadows, the last actually taking their name from a suggestion made by Harris.

A charismatic figure, whose very on-stage presence was enough to guarantee considerable excitement among the female members of The Shadows' audience, it wasn't all that surprising when Jet decided to go his own way in 1962, cutting a brace of high-flying singles in 'Besame Mucho' and 'Theme From The Man With The Golden Arm', the latter getting banned by the Beeb because of its drug connotations.

And the following year saw the Harris career initially moving further up as the six-string Fender bassman got together with Tony Meehan, their combination of twang and bang providing three Top Five singles – 'Diamonds', 'Scarlett O'Hara' and 'Applejack'.

But whatever Harris' qualifications as a musician, he seemed even more at home as a hellraiser. He appeared in a Brighton court on a drunk and disorderly charge, got involved in a car crash, assaulted one man and was found by police pointing a shotgun at some people in the block of flats

Jet Harris with his wife in the seventies

in which he lived. 'On the face of it, this looks like real mental trouble,' the magistrate observed.

A second road accident, in September 1963, in which Harris' chauffeur-driven car collided with a bus near Evesham, was the clincher. Both Jet and his girl-friend, singer Billie Davis, were badly injured, and Harris' nerves seemed to snap like one of his guitar-strings. For a while he disappeared from the music scene. In 1964, with the aid of the Stones' Brian Jones, Harris tried to piece things together once more and get back on the road. But a February concert at Edmonton Granada proved a disaster, Jet muffing all his intros, failing to complete three of the four numbers played and eventually walking offstage after the opening chords of 'Big Bad Bass'. Other comeback attempts fared little better, and it was obvious that Harris was finished as a top-flight musician. Soon the £1,000 a week man could be found asphalting roads for a hundredth of that wage. His marriage went on the rocks, and a second one that followed did likewise. He still played bass-guitar from time to time and during the summers of 1970–74 played dates in Jersey. The winters brought more menial jobs, and Harris worked variously as a bricklayer, chef, logger, fisherman, hospital porter and, in a private venture, as a cockles and whelks seller. For a while he was employed as a barman, then in 1974 turned up in Cheltenham where he lived in a caravan and found employment as a bus-conductor for a Bristol-based company. It couldn't last – and didn't. Jet was soon sacked after an argument with a passenger.

It was in April, 1975, that things took a turn for the better. It was then that Harris got married for the third time, to a Scottish nurse named Margaret, an occasion which caused him to grant an interview during which he declared: 'I've got no money left. It all went on cars, birds and booze. The car crash shook me up horribly. I became a physical wreck and turned to the bottle . . . or rather two bottles of vodka a day.'

For a while it seemed that Jet might be on the way back. Later that year he recorded his first single in yonks, an instrumental called, appropriately 'Theme For A Fallen Idol'. He lined up a few dates in the company of the revived

Tornados and even acquired a brand new fan club.

It was too late in the day, though. Even curiosity value couldn't keep the new Harris career afloat. Before long, he was back to the odd-job and occasional gig formula once more, his most recent non-musical vocation being as repairer of Space Invader machines.

On rock's snakes and ladders board Jet Harris is the guy who nearly made it to the last square, only to slip down that python which dangles its tailend back in square one.

Maybe his current involvement with old partner Tony Meehan and songwriter Jerry Lordan will see him breaking the jinx at last.

The Herd

IF NOTHING ELSE, The Herd spawned a true, up-to-his-boots-in-golden-discs type superstar in vocalist-guitarist Peter Frampton. Initially though, it seemed they wouldn't amount to much. For when Frampers, a schoolmate of David Bowie's, got together with Andy Bown (keyboards), Gary Taylor (bass) and Andy Steele (drums) and set out to entrance the London club scene in early '65, their records, for Parlophone, generally sank without trace. Then Alan Blaikley and Ken Howard, the songwriting team who'd given The Honeycombs and Dave Dee, Dozy, Beaky, Mick and Tich a leg-up, moved in to mastermind The Herd's pop progress. After which, in 1967, following a switch to the Fontana label, came a brace of hits, 'From The Underworld' and 'Paradise Lost', followed by one in the spring of '68, 'I Don't Want Our Loving To Die' – all of which meant that the weekly wage of each band member was raised to the grand sum of £15!

The exposure provided by the three hits resulted in Frampton becoming the face that launched a thousand teenybop mags. *Rave* even went as far as voting him the 'Face of '68', a fact which was usually referred to in every Frampton review or interview for the next ten years.

But, despite the band's popularity and Frampton's assertion that 'I'm lucky to be able to pursue my hobby and make money doing it', The Herd began falling apart.

Andy Steele was the first to quit, the reason being listed as ill-health. Then Frampton nipped off to form Humble Pie, leaving Bown, Taylor and replacement drummer Henry Spinetti (brother of actor Victor Spinetti) to survive just one

final unsuccessful single.

It was at this stage, as anyone in W. H. Smith's record department will tell you, that Peter Frampton began moving further up the ladder, cutting a number of albums with Humble Pie, playing the famous gig in Hyde Park ('The best I've ever done' – Frampton, 1973) and splitting from the band in 1971 to go his own way. Eventually he even quit Beckenham for New York, where he'd got 'a lovely lady' waiting and recorded 'Frampton Comes Alive', a 1975 album that tore the American charts to shreds, selling in excess of four million copies, and also begetting 'Show Me The Way', a single that charted just about everywhere in the universe.

Since that time, Frampton's continued putting out a series of high-selling albums for A&M, along with a fair flow of punter-pulling singles. Also, in 1978, he became something of a movie star, teaming up with The Bee Gees to appear in *Sgt Pepper's Lonely Hearts Club Band*, a would-be blockbuster of a film based on the music of The Beatles. All-in-all then, things haven't worked out too badly for 'The Face of '68', even though his 1979 album 'Where Should I Be' disclosed the fact that, despite his wealth, the Frampton personal life had gone sadly awry, one song, 'It's A Sad Affair', relating to a break-up with his long-time girl friend.

In the interim, Andy Bown has put in his fair share of rock-slog, first forming Judas Jump – a band that also included drummer Spinetti – before becoming part of Storyteller and, in 1972, heading off to get involved in a solo career. This, in truth, hasn't added up to all that much. It's resulted in, as one pundit would have it, 'five less-than-platinum albums', plus a handful of singles, one of which, 'Another Shipwreck', was one of my favourite pop records during 1979. One way or another though, Andy Bown's a musician who may never make a great deal of money as a solo performer but his work as a session man and as an auxiliary member of Status Quo, with whom he has appeared on record and stage, means he can sleep nights without counting overdrafts.

Gary Taylor's also lasted the course since The Herd split, having appeared on an abundance of studio sessions and toured with likes of Gerry Rafferty, while Andy Steele too has appeared on albums by numerous artists, including Gerry Rafferty, Laurie Styvers and Clifford T. Ward. The Herd, then, have done okay. One worldbeating winner and no real losers. A lot of other now-defunct sixties bands would have settled for less.

Herman's Hermits

PETER NOONE'S DAD rang me up one day during 1980 and asked if I could tell him where he could obtain a copy of his son's latest album.

'Young Peter's been living in the States for some time,' he said, 'and he told me that he'd formed a band called The Tremblers, but I can't get a copy of his album anywhere. It was different in the sixties. I remember him working with that Lulu. She was all right, wasn't she?'

And certainly it *was* different in the sixties for the babyfaced Noone. Then he was Herman, leader of The Hermits, an outfit that not only chalked up seventeen British hits but also cleaned up on the other side of the Atlantic to the tune of fourteen biggies, including two Number Ones.

Peter Noone was all of sixteen when The Hermits, who'd formerly been The Heartbeats, first met up with producer Mickie Most. The band then comprised Noone (vocals), Keith Hopwood (guitar), Derek Leckenby (guitar), Karl Green (bass) and Barry Whitwam (drums) and it was this unit that Most took into the studio to record 'I'm Into Something Good', a cheerful earful that took Herman to the top of the British charts and sparked off the greatest display of molar power ever to confront a British TV audience. Herman was really George Formby in a beat group setting, just the sort of Lancashire lad they'd love down at The Rover's Return.

And lots of other folk loved him too, for his records couldn't be pressed up fast enough, right from 1964 through to 1970, 'I'm Into Something Good' proving a precursor to a flow of smash successes that included 'Silhouettes', 'Wonderful World', 'A Must To Avoid', 'No Milk Today',

'There's A Kind Of Hush', 'Something's Happening', 'My Sentimental Friend' and 'Years May Come, Years May Go'. Meanwhile, in the States, even Herman's version of 'Henry The Eighth I Am', reached the top spot – which proved just how much they were prepared to take to show how deeply they cared for him.

And America did care. So much so that Hollywood decided Herman and The Hermits should be movie stars. Which is why the band grabbed top credits on such tinsel town productions as *Hold On* and *Mrs Brown You've Got A Lovely Daughter*, while also edging their way into a couple of other celluloid song-parades.

'The reason we made it in America,' Herman later told *NME*'s Tony Stewart, 'was because I was like a little schoolboy. When I was there they asked me to do all these radio and TV shows and everybody heard the accent and thought I was cute.'

But Herman was growing up to be Peter Noone. During the late sixties he and the band began disagreeing upon direction.

'They weren't growing and I wanted to be out there with the energy,' he complained. He began using his real name for solo work and in mid-1971 Peter Noone and The Hermits parted company. 'Not many people are aware that we have not released an album for four years purely because we could not mutually agree on material,' he stated at the time. 'With only myself to worry about I can broaden my repertoire.'

The first Peter Noone solo single came out in mid-'71. Titled 'Oh You Pretty Thing' it was penned by David Bowie and produced by Mickie Most for release on his own RAK label. A major hit in Britain, it augured well for the Noone solo career. But it was a one-off. By 1973 Noone was back to being Herman, leading The Hermits on an American tour along with Gerry And The Pacemakers, Billy J. Kramer And The Dakotas, The Searchers and Wayne Fontana And The Mindbenders.

'We even sold out Madison Square Garden – which Herman's Hermits had never done in the sixties when they were big,' he enthused to *Goldmine*'s Jeff Tamarkin, also expressing some bewilderment about being considered an oldie at the age of twenty-four!

In 1974 he and his French wife turned up in Britain once more, Noone explaining that even if he was no longer making successful records he was still pulling in royalties from his past hits, a recent cheque being for a modest five grand! These days he tends to gloss over the non-event that the seventies were for him. 'I think I was waiting for the eighties. Waiting for Nick Lowe, Dave Edmunds and Elvis Costello, people who would be prepared to work hard for their money and not just arrive on stage in a space ship. The seventies were all about arriving on stage with big powerful amplifiers – the Led Zeppelin years.'

Certainly Noone did little during this period, spending some years laying low in France and cutting but three singles over a lengthy period before reaching a point where he admitted to be 'barely surviving'. The eighties *did* bring a change in fortunes. He gained some TV work in America, began leading a band known as The Tremblers, who signed a deal with producer Bruce Johnston's label and released an album called 'Twice Nightly' which came packed with contemporary pop material, including an Elvis Costello song called 'Green Shirt'. By 1982 The Tremblers were no more and Peter Noone, who'd taken over the role of Frederick in the touring production of *The Pirates Of Penzance*, moved on to make a solo album titled 'One Of The Glory Boys'. More recently he's returned to Britain to appear in the London version of *The Pirates* and grab his share of the glory once again. And who's to say he won't? After all, it isn't easy to write off someone who's sold over fifty million records.

Though they haven't worked with Peter Noone since 1973, Herman's Hermits still exist. The foursome put out a Pye single called 'Heart Get Ready For Love' in early 1978. Green, Leckenby and Whitwam were still within, Keith Hopwood having been replaced by Frank Renshaw.

'Since then, Karl has left,' says Derek Leckenby. 'By the spring of 1980 he'd had enough of life on the road and just wanted to settle down with his wife and have a family. Since then he's started his own tiling business – though he still does a bit of writing, sometimes working with Rick Lee of Ten

Years After. Barry Whitwam's still with the band but we've got a new bass-player in Paul Farnell, who joined in May, 1981. And Garth Elliott is our front man these days. He was with Alvin Stardust and The Swinging Blue Jeans. He plays rhythm guitar and also writes lots of new stuff for us. These days we're very American musically – our sound is mainly heavy West Coast rock. And one reason that we're so American is that between 1973 and 1981 we spent ninety-nine per cent of our time commuting to the States. We don't work a lot in England. We don't kid ourselves – there aren't that many places we can play here. So it's mainly overseas things – we've got trips to Australia and Scandinavia lined up this year. Also we're doing Germany in the company of The Equals. We keep pretty busy.'

The Honeybus

'**I** CAN'T LET MAGGIE GO' was the only hit The Honeybus ever floated our way. I say 'floated' because every time I hear the song these days I have a mental vision of that hot-air balloon heading skywards on my television screen. I guess Pete Dello must have sold a lot of Nimble bread in his time.

But in my view 'Do I Figure In Your Life', which preceded 'Maggie' was an all-time cracker. A great song, and in my book it's still a hit.

The story of The Honeybus is short if not sweet. Basically, there were four guys – Pete Dello, a guitarist/singer/songwriter, whose real name was Blumson; Ray Cane, a bassist from Hackney, whose real name was Byart; and Peter Kircher (drums) and Colin Hare (guitar) who could only afford the names they were born with. They got together and gained a Deram recording contract, made a single called 'Delighted To See You', which immediately went into hiding, then followed up with 'Do I Figure In Your Life' and 'I Can't Let Maggie Go', two of the tastiest singles of 1967 and 1968 respectively. 'We want to build slowly,' claimed Terry Noon, the band's manager. 'We're not going to knock ourselves out and wear ourselves into the ground recording new material and playing every date offered. We want to create something and we want to do it our way. If we fail, at least we haven't killed ourselves doing it.'

The band did fail. Soon after, in fact. Almost immediately after the success of 'Maggie', Pete Dello, the song's composer and singer, threw in the towel. And though he was quickly replaced by Jim Kelly, a Scot whom they'd first met while playing clubs in Germany, The Honeybus just didn't mean anything with Dello gone. A few records later they'd gone – for good.

Terry Noon is still part of the music scene. Today he's head of a music publishing company known as Noon Music. And he still has fond memories of The Honeybus. 'It all began when Pete Dello and I played together in an outfit known as Steve Derbyshire And The Yum Yum Band – the regular band at Tiles, the club in London's Oxford Street. Afterwards I moved into publishing but Pete and I still used to get together and have a coffee from time to time. One day he said: "If I set up a band, will you manage it?" I said I would and, if I remember rightly, I put a couple of hundred pounds into the project. All went well at first. We had a deal with Deram, had a turntable hit with "Do I Figure In Your Life" and then had a really big hit with "I Can't Let Maggie Go". The trouble with being successful was that The Honeybus were expected to tour more, make more trips to the Continent and so forth. Pete wasn't into all that sort of thing, he was more into songwriting and working in the studio. He just didn't want to be a pop star. I remember we did an Oxford gig once where the girls went bananas over the band. Pete just hated it all – though the other boys liked it. Eventually he just left and the band carried on without him for a while. One single "Girl Of Independent Means", written by Ray Cane, got into one Top Thirty and the band's "Story" album had some excellent things on it. But to be honest, though the band were good in the studio and did many adventurous things – they were one of the first bands to use a string quartet on a radio broadcast – they weren't all that good onstage. About a year after Pete left I had to call them all together and ask them if they shouldn't call it a day. "Look," I said, "You've got a great reputation but you can either carry on and prostitute the band's name or you can pack it in while you're still highly respected." They decided to pack it in, the split was amicable and we all remained friends.'

Both Ray Cane and Colin Hare are currently out of the music business, says Noon, 'But Pete Kircher is still very much a part of it, being the drummer with Status Quo.'

But what of Pete Dello – who to all intents and purposes *was* Honeybus? 'I did several Decca deals for Pete and there was also an album for WEA though it didn't come out because it really wasn't up to expectations. Around 1973 there was a Pete Dello and Friends album though – it came out on the Nepentha label, through Phonogram. Pete called it "Into Your Ears" and it was a very fine album. Ray Coleman of the *Melody Maker* nominated it as best album of the year. One of the songs on the album is "I'm A Gambler", which Pete wrote just after he left Honeybus. If he had stayed with the band then it would have been the follow-up to "I Can't Let Maggie Go" and I'm certain that had Pete stayed with the band and they had recorded "I'm A Gambler" then things would have gone on a lot longer because they were a fine band and "Gambler" was an excellent song. Several people have covered it and Pete's done it himself a couple of times but if Honeybus had done it then, it would have been as big as "Maggie".

'Pete did reform The Honeybus, just for recording sessions, at one point,' remembers Noon. 'He got all the original members back together again and made some sides for Bell, songs like "The Lady's Not For Burning". There was also another stab at "I'm A Gambler" made under the name of Magneta, for Arista, with Ray Cane as producer. Pete's songs have done very well over the years. Kate Taylor, James Taylor's sister, did a version of "Do I Figure In Your Life?" on an album which was a massive seller and lots of other people have done the song. Also there was that "I Can't Let Maggie Go" TV commercial – at one time, it was one of the longest running ads on television. Eventually they replaced it with a song that sounded almost identical. Pete still writes and still brings songs in to me from time to time, though I haven't used any recently. But he's a very talented writer and I'm certain he'll come up with something again. Really, I can't understand why he never had a massive hit with "I'm A Gambler".'

Above: *Peter Sarstedt*
Below: *Eden Kane*

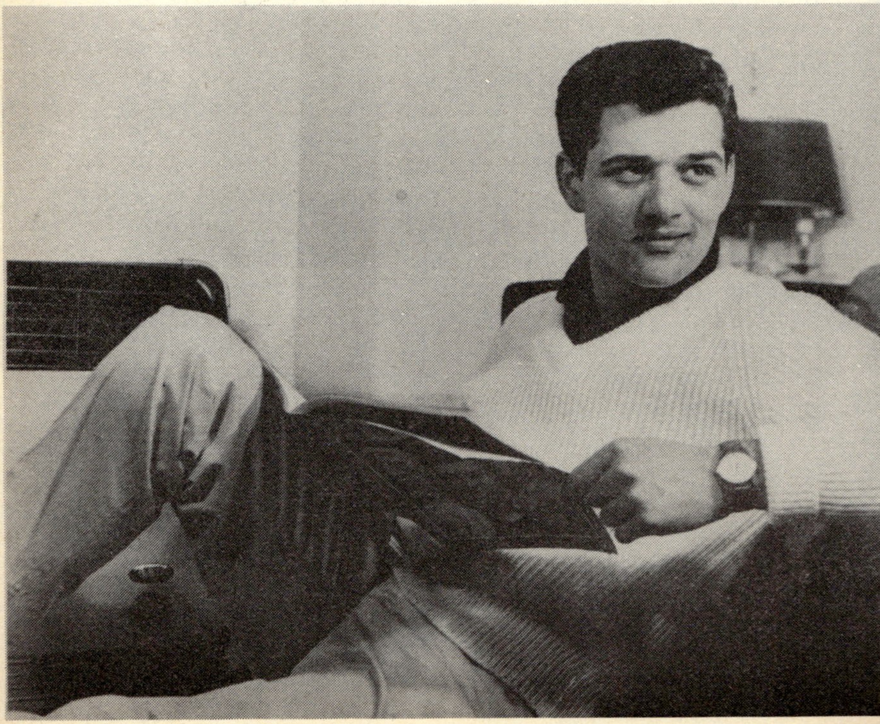

Eden Kane
and Peter Sarstedt

IN EARLY 1961, Eden Kane, then eighteen, was playing the working men's club circuit in places like Sheffield and Leeds, usually providing a vocal interlude between bouts of bingo. 'My managers said they were giving me my national service in show-biz and, believe me, they weren't kidding,' he later claimed.

The Delhi-born singer wasn't quite an overnight success – though very nearly. He turned up in London to audition for the role of Birdie in the musical 'Bye Bye, Birdie' but lost out to Marty Wilde. Even a recording contract with Pye brought little in the way of kudos.

However, signed to Decca, he recorded a Johnny Worth song called 'Well, I Ask You', which zoomed to the top of the nation's charts with some alacrity during the summer of '61. Three more huge hits followed during '61 and '62 – 'Get Lost', 'Forget Me Not' and 'I Don't Know Why I Love You Like I Do'. Then, just as everyone was getting ready to write him off, he signed for Fontana Records and came up with 'Boys Cry', a 1964 winner that put him back in the heart-throb stakes once more.

But the fickleness of youth wasn't going to be denied. After 'Boys Cry', no one ever wanted to buy his records again. Not ever.

Strange really, for Kane, whose real name was Richard Graham Sarstedt, was dark, handsome in a macho way and possessed the kind of sexy growl of a voice that augured well for a long future in pop. But maybe he was born under the wrong sign or something for not only did his records cease to sell, he also flunked out in the world of finance, losing much of the cash he'd made on his hits when a company in which he'd invested crashed, leaving him penniless for a time.

However, if one Sarstedt flopped, there was another to take his place. Richard's younger brother Peter stepped up to revive the family fortunes with the folksy 'Where Do You Go To My Lovely?' in 1969, following it with the only slightly less successful 'Frozen Orange Juice'.

Eden, in the meantime, had become Rick Sarstedt once more and headed out to Australia for a couple of years. Later, he moved to Los Angeles, married an American girl, who gave him a daughter, and, during his five years' stay on the US West Coast, made a living by singing in various bars and clubs. It was 1973 that he turned up in London again, teaming up with Peter and his other brother, Robin, to record an album called 'Worlds Apart Together'. It was during the promo-drive on this album that Peter took it upon himself to explain to journalist Andrew Furnival exactly why things had gone wrong for Rick. 'He was never liked by the boys because he went for the girls. You only had to start something like that with the girls and the boys would be waiting for you afterwards. Guys would be running around with iron bars trying to smash down the door of the dressing room and beat him up. It went on like that for a few years and then it just stopped. There was no more urgency for the Eden Kane myth or whatever it was. He was still the same guy. It was just that everything else which had kept him there, suddenly collapsed.' When the brothers' collective effort failed to make much impression on record buyers, the threesome went their separate ways once again, Robin – who's also recorded under the names of Clive Sands and Clive Sarstedt – popped up in 1976 with a revival of Hoagy Carmichael's 'My Resistance Is Low' that climbed to Number Three in the British charts. So, over a period spanning fifteen years, all three Sarstedts had logged Top Ten solo singles in the UK – something that even The Bee Gees have yet failed to achieve.

These days Peter Sarstedt, he of the black bushy mop and resplendent moustache, is not doing at all badly. After a lengthy stay in Copenhagen, he's resident in Britain once more and lives in a Wiltshire farmhouse with his wife, an American girl called Joanna.

His musical career has had its ups and downs during the seventies. The flop Sarstedt Brothers album of '73 was followed by solo albums for such companies as Warner Brothers and Ariola Hansa — both patchy but containing the odd, brilliantly inventive song. (The *Melody Maker* wrote of 'Beirut', a song from Peter's 'PS' album: 'The great thing about this wonderful song is that the story is unfinished. Play it twenty times and you're still intrigued.')

In 1981 Peter played a Barbican centre concert and has since continued with a policy of playing just a few good dates each year rather than a string of second-rate ones. He's had a near-hit single with 'Love Among The Ruins', which scraped along the bottom of the charts in '82 — and 1983 he completed work on a TV film which featured Sarstedt singing against settings shot in Copenhagen, Paris, London and Iceland. Also in 1983 Rick/Richard/Eden returned from another stay in Los Angeles to attend Billy Fury's funeral and also chomp over the possibility of a second Sarstedt brothers get-together. 'Last time it wasn't handled properly,' claims their management. 'Maybe this time we'll get it right.' Either way, for Eden Kane it's got to be a hell of a lot better than all those bingo session gigs in deepest Yorkshire.

Billy J. Kramer

MERSEYBEAT RAN RIOT in 1963. The Beatles, Gerry And The Pacemakers, and The Searchers all had Number One hits that year and, together with one other act, ensured that between April and December, Scouse acts held onto the top position for no less than thirty-seven weeks.

The 'one other act' was Billy J. Kramer, leader of The Dakotas (a band that came from Manchester), whose 'Bad To Me' stayed at Number One for three weeks, proving an unstoppable follow-up to Kramer's first chart success, 'Do You Want To Know A Secret', a version of a song on The Beatles' first album. Billy J. or William Howard Ashton to give him his original name, was the son of a Liverpool docker. A British Rail worker, his was an everyday kind of voice, the sort probably shared by a legion of Liverpool linemen. But he sang with a local band, called The Coasters, one night after somebody nicked his guitar and he was left with nothing else to do. And somehow or another he became so popular that Brian Epstein signed him and linked him with The Dakotas.

As with the case of so many Epstein-managed bands, they were handed a Beatles track with which to make their mark and duly did their duty by 'Do You Want To Know A Secret', making all concerned very happy and a mite more welcome at any bank. The line-up at that point in the band's career was Kramer (vocals), Mike Maxfield (lead guitar), Robin McDonald (rhythm guitar), Ray Jones (bass) and Tony Mansfield, brother of Elkie Brooks, (drums) – though changes were to ensue even while The Dakotas were at the top. Which wasn't long.

For, just five hits and a couple of years after 'Do You Want To Know A Secret' – the five hits being 'Bad To Me', 'I'll Keep You Satisfied', 'Little Children' (another Number One), 'From A Window' and 'Trains And Boats And Planes' – the name of Billy J. Kramer disappeared from the charts, never to be seen again. It was in 1966, in the wake of three flop singles, that Kramer and The Dakotas finally parted company, Billy picking up a couple of different backing groups en route but failing to change his luck. Eventually his big weekly date was on a kids' TV show called *Lift Off*, though he continued cutting the odd single or two, changing his style to suit the times. But nothing happened that seemed likely to make him a main man once again. Nevertheless, the club dates still flowed in and during 1973 he even flew to the States to appear in Richard Nader's sixties revival tour. Further tours in Australia, Europe and the USA helped keep Kramer busy during the mid-seventies while guest appearances on such TV shows as *Supersonic*, *Arrows* and *Pop At Mill*, along with the usual flurry of club gigs, ensured that his face was not forgotten by the British public.

By 1977 it just seemed possible that he might climb a few rungs up the ladder again – for he was once more signed by EMI, the company with which he'd recorded during his chart-topping era.

I bumped into him around that time. He'd just recorded a single called 'San Diego' and was crossing his fingers in anticipation of its success. It seemed that he was then living near Daventry and was quite comfortably off from his appearances on the club circuit but was still really hoping for that one hit record that had eluded him since 1965. He said then that he didn't think all that much musically of his earlier successes and felt that he was better equipped vocally in the seventies than when he was leading The Dakotas.

Unfortunately, neither 'San Diego' nor its follow-up, 'Ships That Pass In The Night', did much for Billy J., whose middle initial, by the way, doesn't stand for anything in particular – 'It was a Lennon idea, just to round the name off'. So nothing has changed. He continues to make singles – recent ones have come out on labels like Hobo, JM and Runaway — while his name still appears on the bills at my local club from time to time. In fact, he's doing all right and at least hasn't had to face the unemployment crisis that has left millions of others without hope and a distinct lack of the readies. In that way he's lucky.

He knows it too. Once it was reported that he was thinking of switching his name back to Billy Ashton in order to make a fresh start to his career. But as he told *NME* just a few years ago: 'With my work, I think it's a bonus having a name that's already established. It's not a hang-up. What could possibly be a hang-up about having records that sold millions and millions? Some people work all their lives and their names are never heard of. I'm a very lucky person and if I never achieve success again, I will still have done a lot with my life.'

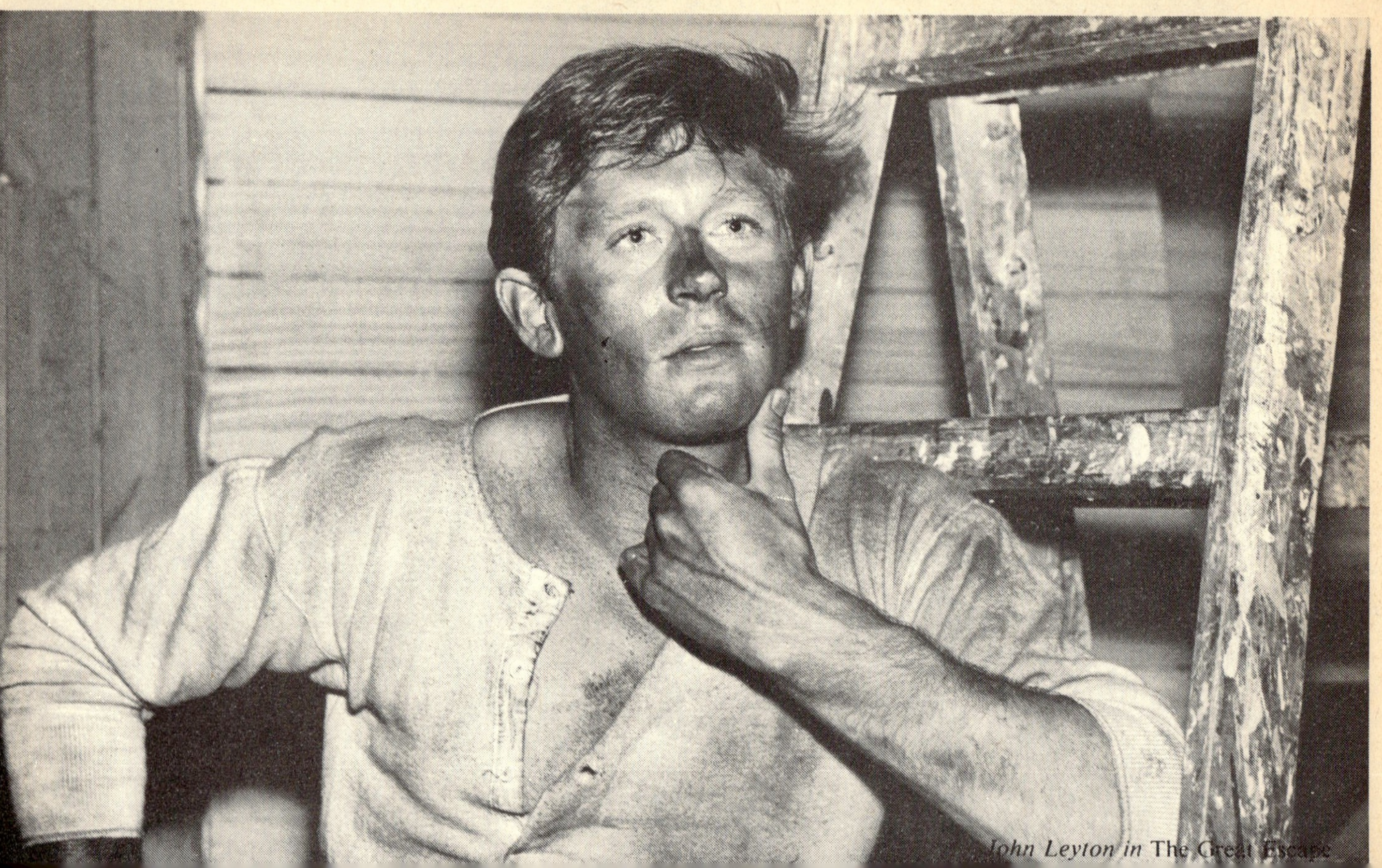

John Leyton in The Great Escape

John Leyton

L EYTON'S WHOLE MUSICAL career was sparked by just one appearance on a TV soap opera. In mid-'61, the tall, fair-headed good-looker took the role of Johnny St Cyr, a singer appearing in the series *Harper's West One* and sang 'Johnny Remember Me'. The ill-fated Top Rank label issued the number on a single just four days later and the result was sheer pandemonium.

The TV company was inundated with enquiries about the young actor, whose biggest previous role had been as Ginger in the *Biggles* TV series, and the record shops suffered from a massive influx of Leyton lovers as soon as the record graced their racks.

By the end of August it was Number One in the *Record Mirror* charts and there it remained for the next three weeks, eventually surrendering its hallowed spot to The Shadows' 'Kon-Tiki'.

Leyton, an actor born in Frinton-on-Sea, had spent some time in York Repertory Theatre, where he'd met his manager Robert Stigwood. Soon he had another winner with his follow-up single, 'Wild Wind' and then completed his hat-trick of hits for the year with 'Son, This Is She'.

Massive in terms of popularity, he set out on a three month tour with Billy Fury, sang 'Lonely City' in the film *It's Trad Dad*, gained a major role in the blockbusting *The Great Escape* and continued logging various chart hits through to 1964, in which year, while still bigger than The Rolling Stones – on Leyton's final concert tour, he topped the bill while Jagger and his mates merely closed the first half of the show – he quit the music biz and emigrated to America, there marrying an English-born girl named Dini.

At the time, it seemed a logical move to make. His screen career was flourishing and sales of his records were slowly diminishing. He got out while the going was good. And when he was signed to play alongside Frank Sinatra in *Von Ryan's Express* during 1965, everyone nodded and said just how shrewd Leyton had been.

In 1966, he starred in *Jericho*, a sixteen-episode American TV series about a spy team that operated behind enemy lines, and then grabbed a part in the 1968 Cinerama epic *Krakatoa, East Of Java*, playing second fiddle to a tidal wave. Certainly the tide was beginning to turn for John Leyton. In 1973, he sold his house in Malibu and returned to Britain, where he announced: 'There is a slump in the film industry in America which has persuaded me that it was time to get out of Hollywood and do something different.'

Something different meant getting back into music once more. He'd met up with songwriter Kenny Young, who encouraged Leyton to reactivate his career as a pop vocalist. A deal was set up and an album plus a couple of singles materialised on the York label during 1973–74. Not that anyone noticed. The sales register stayed in the zilch position and news coverage was minimal.

These days Leyton regards himself as an actor who merely got into the recording business by way of a lucky accident. He still turns up from time to time on TV – recently he appeared in an HTV series titled *The Square Leopard* – and spends a considerable portion of his life in the world of film production and finance. He received no financial benefit from his initial foray into the world of pop – like many others he found that all his royalties had to be paid into the hands of the Official Receiver after the death of Joe Meek, producer of his many hits – and it's only in recent times that he's regained the rights to all his old material. Another of his ventures involves a chain of eating houses, which seems to be turning nosh into cash in enviable style. And one wonders if the coffee served in these establishments is dubbed Von Ryan's Expresso. Then again, maybe not.

Love Affair

'**H**I, FRED! Rock star joins Jaffa squad – Morgan-Fisher flips lid!' So began a letter that came my way at the fag end of '81. At least it explained where one member of Love Affair had ended up. In Brussels, apparently, and momentarily considering quitting music-biz while he 'got involved with the orange-clad followers of a guru called Bhagwam Shree Rajneesh.' Morgan-Fisher became a member of Love Affair when they first got together back in '66. He was the keyboardist and 16-year-old Steve Ellis was the vocalist, while the rest of the band consisted of Rex Brayley (guitar), Mick Jackson (bass) and Mo Bacon (drums). Initially they played the London club scene, gained something of a reputation and eventually went professional – at which point Fisher headed back to college for a while, his replacement being Lynton Guest. Success came easy at that stage. They – or rather Steve Ellis plus a number of sessionmen – recorded a song called 'Everlasting Love' and had it issued through CBS, even though the label hadn't actually signed them – an oversight that was hastily rectified when the disc shot to Number One in January, 1968. There were two more hits that year – 'Rainbow Valley' and 'A Day Without Love' – after which Morgan-Fisher rejoined the band in time for such 1969 winners as 'One Road' and 'Bringing On Back The Good Times'.

Then Steve Ellis quit to form his own band, Ellis: the hits were tapering off and he claimed that he'd received little in the way of financial gain to show for his efforts on behalf of Love Affair – 'Things were often so bad we used to hold down the road manager and help ourselves to the cash'. He

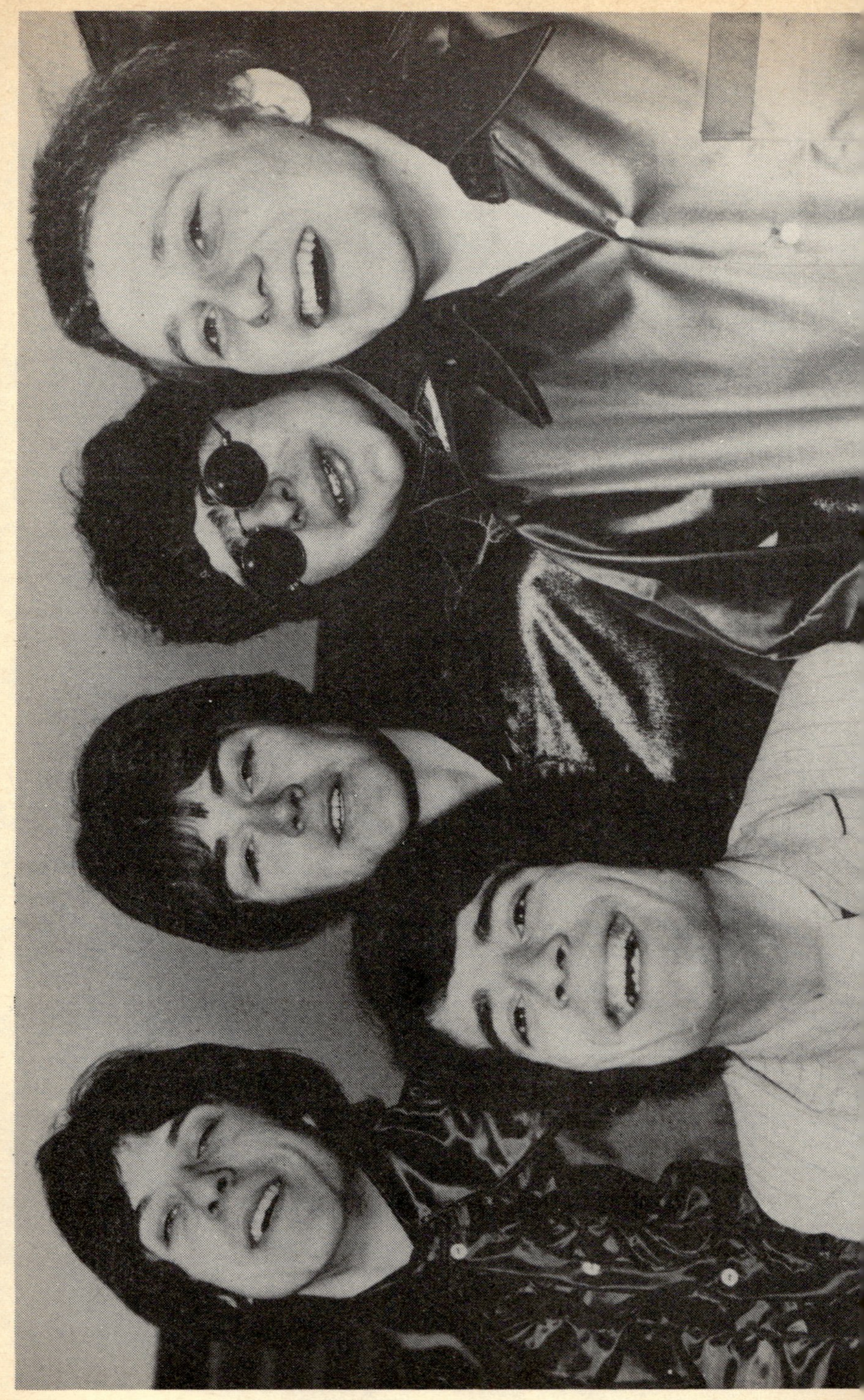

was followed by Morgan-Fisher and Bacon (whose father had managed the band from the onset) who went off to form a band called Morgan. But still Love Affair, fielding an ever-changing flood of replacements, continued gigging throughout the early seventies, generally finding their fill of dates on the club and cabaret circuit. However, by this time the band had become so faceless that Steve Ellis, in a *Zig Zag* interview, opined that there were at least three different Love Affairs on the road. And, with all the known members gone, it was at least a possibility.

Even after the death of manager Sid Bacon in 1974, Love Affair still continued on their rounds, Mo Bacon returning to take over the reins of management. In the interim, Steve Ellis had little luck with Ellis. The band made a couple of albums for CBS during 1972–73 then split, Steve moving on to provide vocals for the much heralded but equally unsuccessful Widowmaker, an outfit headed by ex-Mott The Hoople man Ariel Bender. After that he dropped out of sight, only to be remembered whenever a TV company screened *Loot*, the film version of the Joe Orton play, which featured some songs by the one-time boy wonder.

Disenchanted with the knocks he had received from the music business, Ellis opted for a more everyday lifestyle but was the victim of ill fate once more when, while labouring, he was badly injured in an accident with a fork-lift truck, one of his feet being severely crushed.

'He's a lot better now,' claims Mo Bacon, who recently masterminded Ellis's return to music and his first TV appearance for many years, on the series *Greatest Hits*. 'He's been recording with the aid of Overend Watts and Dale Griffin, both ex-Mott The Hoople, and sounds as great as ever.'

Any history of Love Affair inevitably leads to a mention of Mott The Hoople. It was the band that Morgan-Fisher joined after the failure of Morgan. Later, after Mott split, he helped them reform as British Lions, a venture which didn't quite work out as planned. Later, in 1979, he formed his own record company, Pipe Records, for which he produced 'Hybrid Kids', an album that purported to be a sampler by thirteen new wave bands – though, in reality, every note had been played by Morgan-Fisher, who'd recorded the whole thing in his Notting Hill flat at a cost of just thirty pounds!

He followed this with 'Miniatures', a fifty-one track album by various musicians and personalities, all of whom were given no more than a minute each in which to do their respective things, and 'Claws', undoubtedly the world's most unusual Christmas album. But though these and other weird but often wonderful records brought the one-time Finchley Mod a fair amount of critical acclaim, if little in the way of rent money, he eventually decided that enough was enough. Boredom set in and he departed for India, his experiences in that country encouraging him to find a place in the guru's establishment in Belgium.

'He's been to America since then,' reports Bacon. 'Morgan lived in Oregon for a while, though the last I heard he'd returned to London and was living with his sister Caroline. He's still very much involved in music and was keyboardist on Queen's 1982 world tour, though I'm not certain what he's up to right now.' Recalling his renewed association with Steve Ellis, Bacon says: 'I hadn't spoken to him for years but I'd heard he was living down in Brighton. I had to go down that way to visit some friends, so I gave Steve a call. And when he answered the door he said: "Funny you should come round here – I was just thinking of doing something again and was about to give you a call." Of the other original members of Love Affair, Mick Jackson is doing really well. He was always into cars and these days he has a big car leasing firm up in Bradford. But Rex Bayley – well, I don't know what's happened to him. There's still a Love Affair though – and Martin Lyon, who's the singer with the band now, is the all-time longest surviving member. He's been with Love Affair for over nine years – while people like myself and Steve were only with the band for three or four years. Me – I'm still running the original management company that we had. But we also do records, run an agency and we're also into films. It's become a kind of Bacon empire!'

Cathy McGowan

THE SEVENTIES BEGAN in auspicious style for Cathy McGowan.

'Ex-TV pop girl Cathy McGowan and film actor Hywel Bennett obviously have no time for long engagements' read the caption on a lovey-dovey photograph that a publicist sent my way. 'Hywel proposed last Friday and on Saturday she accepted. And next Saturday, January 17, they will be married.' At the same time, Hywel told the press: 'We've known each other for four years. Love grew naturally. During that time neither of us went out with anyone else seriously. Marriage had to come.'

The funny thing was that McGowan, who had no talent than that which enabled her to be herself, had a face that was even better known than Bennett's, even though he had already appeared in such films as *The Family Way*, *Twisted Nerve* and *The Virgin Soldiers*. She'd come from almost out of nowhere and became compere on *Ready, Steady, Go!* the biggest TV pop show to emerge from the sixties. In some ways she was awful. Just a Mod, with a fringe that fell down below her eyes. And no poise whatsoever. She stumbled over her intros, called everyone and everything 'smashin'' or 't'rific' and practically fell over her pointy shoes every time a hero like Dave Clark put in an appearance on the show. But her sheer amateurism made her a star. She was everyone's kid sister, albeit one with a lucky streak. If she could make it, there was hope for us all.

Not that she stayed ordinary. When Rediffusion amalgamated with ABC in 1968 and *Ready, Steady, Go!* was taken off, the 'one-time Queen Of The Mods' as one paper

described her, moved on to head her own teenage clothes empire, pulling in £50,000 a year. Then she married Hywel Bennett after borrowing Cilla Black's wedding-ring, explaining: 'Cilla and I rushed around all day trying to buy a plain gold ring. But they were all too flashy, so Cilla's lending me hers.'

Despite the birth of a daughter, the marriage fell apart in 1975 and the then 31-year-old McGowan opted out of public life, never to face a reporter again.

I would have loved her to have penned a foreword to this book. For, to many, Cathy McGowan, along with the Beatles and Carnaby Street, *was* the sixties. I mentioned this to her sister, well-known journalist Frankie McGowan, who explained: 'Cathy has been approached by lots of people to do things connected with the sixties but she never agrees to do them. If you look through the cuttings file at any newspaper you won't find anything about her that's appeared over the past ten years. She just wants to forget show-biz now. However, I'll give you a number and you can put your suggestion if you like.'

Later, I contacted Cathy McGowan through an intermediary, the latter ringing back to state: 'Cathy says she's sorry and wishes you good luck with the book but feels that her earlier career should now be forgotten.'

And so, Cathy McGowan has elected to become the Garbo of pop, which is sad in a way. She's still to be seen though, sometimes wandering around the shops in the Twickenham-Kingston-upon-Thames area, where she still, apparently, makes her purchases in the name of Cathy Bennett. But does she still say 'smashin'' and 't'rific'?

The Marmalade

Yes, THEY'RE STILL going, though Dylan knows who's in the band right now. At the last checkpoint, founder-member bassist Graham Knight was still around. But the rest of the original Marmalade had long departed in search of pastures banknote-green.

No one expected them to survive all these years anyway. For it was right back in 1961 that the then fourteen-year-old Junior Campbell and his pal Pat Fairie, guitar-toters both, formed a band called The Gaylords, eventually enlisting aid from vocalist Dean Ford, drummer Raymond Duffy and bassist Graham Knight. Hailed as Glasgow's best they pointed their van in the direction of London, made some records – all failures – and then changed their name to The Marmalade, also acquiring a new drummer in Alan Whitehead.

It was May, 1968, when the Great British Public really became aware that The Marmalade existed, notice being served by 'Lovin' Things', a Top Ten single. And if a small proportion of the populace still said 'who?' whenever the band's name was mentioned then this was put right later that same year when Campbell and Co. went for the soft option and recorded The Beatles' 'Ob-La-Di, Ob-La-Da', a ploy that gained them the best selling single in the country.

And so the sixties ended with the band well established and with another couple of chart records, 'Baby Make It Soon' and 'Reflections Of My Life' under their collective belt. Understandably, it seemed that the seventies would present no problem – especially when 'Rainbow', like 'Reflections Of My Life', a Campbell-Ford composition, provided yet another massive-selling single. By 1971, however, the first cracks in the façade appeared. Following another moderate hit with 'My Little One', Junior Campbell, then the band's musical mainman, departed to attend the Royal College of Music. It was a blow, a killer in its way. For Campbell was not only the band's main songwriter but also its producer. Some bands might have considered throwing in the towel at this stage. But The Marmalade merely shrugged their shoulders, brought in yet another song-writing Scot in Hughie Nicholson and carried on as if nothing had occurred. Certainly none of their fans appeared to notice Campbell's departure as Nicholson went to work, providing songs such as 'Cousin Norman', 'Back On The Road' and the sprightly 'Radancer', all hits that kept the Decca presses working at full capacity.

More problems reared their heads. A *News of the World* shock-horror exposé revealed to the world that Marmalade had enjoyed their fill of sexual pleasures while on the road and everyone muttered 'tut-tut' for a while. Others went further and chopped bookings, even Junior Campbell, who had left the band some months earlier, finding that two of his TV appearances had been cancelled within days of the paper's allegations being published. Not as if that was all. Nicholson, the new mainman, had also decided that he'd had enough and went on to join a band named Cody before forming the more successful Blue.

Again the going became tough for the band. Graham Knight opted out and by 1974 only Dean Ford remained from the original line-up. Marmalade still made records but there seemed to be few takers. However, they'd weathered storms before and felt that they could do so again. And they did. With a line-up that once more featured Graham Knight but omitted Dean Ford, who had embarked on a solo career, they signed with Target Records and came up with a single called 'Falling Apart At The Seams' – a title which accurately mirrored the way things were with the band.

Much to the surprise of the pundits, who had long since written Marmalade off, the band had a 1976 Top Ten entry with the disc. Against all odds, they'd once more gotten off the canvas. Such luck couldn't last – and it didn't. Within a short space of time personnel changes ensued once more along with a change of record label. At the tailend of 1979, Marmalade appeared on EMI once more, proffering a one-off single called 'Made In Germany'. This time there was no reprise for the band's fortunes. The record made little impression and it wasn't long before anyone at EMI could even remember the band returning to the fold. Marmalade are still active. If you check a gig sheet, it's possible you'll find them working a club in your area. And Graham Knight's still there to form the link with the past, though it's doubtful you'll be able to put a name to any other members of the group. Still, with well over twenty years gone by since the advent of The Gaylords, little else could be expected. In the interim, original mainman Junior Campbell had prospered. During the early seventies, he recorded two best-selling singles in 'Hallelujah Freedom' and 'Sweet Illusion', also establishing himself as an arranger-producer of quality. Flights with Elton's Rocket Records and the ill-fated Private Stock label have subsequently failed to enhance the Campbell solo career, though his reputation as a producer received a further fillip in 1976 after he talked Barbara Dickson into recording 'Answer Me', the first-ever hit for his fellow-Scot.

Since then, there have been numerous production chores, including a session for Jess Conrad, while Campbell's songs have been performed and recorded by an impressive list of artists.

'One of the most recent was picked up by Frida of Abba,' says Campbell, whom I first interviewed in 1973, when he was living in a luxury Sunningdale home, an establishment guarded by two monster Great Danes. 'That was my first house,' muses Campbell. 'I've since moved to another place, still in Surrey – though now I only have one huge dog!'

That, it appears, is as far as hard times have struck Junior Campbell. But for his fellow leading light in Marmalade, things haven't worked out that well.

'When Dean Ford left the band, he made a solo album for EMI but it didn't do all that well. Afterwards he went out to LA with the Nicholson brothers (Hughie and David) and began sharing a house with them – in fact, they're still living there. But the last I heard was that he was doing decorating or something – which is a bit of a shame.'

The Merseybeats

THEIR NAME SAID it all. Just one glance at that moniker and you knew where they came from and how they sounded. Shrewd that.

Once they'd been The Mavericks and, for a short while, The Pacifics. Then Bob Wooler, MC at The Cavern, suggested they should become The Merseybeats. After which all the right things began to happen for them. Well, sort of. They *were* signed to Brian Epstein, but not for long. He failed to supply them with the same kind of snazzy suits he'd bought for The Beatles. End of artist-management relationship.

They signed a record deal with the Fontana label in 1963 and did a ballad called 'It's Love That Really Counts' that provided them with Top Thirty status right there and then. The media promptly moved into action and within days most teenagers in the land were made aware that The Merseybeats were Tony Crane (lead guitar), Aaron Williams (rhythm guitar), Billy Kinsley (bass) and John Banks (drums).

Their next record became their biggest ever. A lightly-latinised ballad titled 'I Think Of You', it zoomed right into the Top Ten. And though Billy Kinsley decided to leave the band soon after – his replacement being Johnny Gustafson of The Big Three – '64 proved a good year for The Merseybeats who gained two further major hits with 'Don't Turn Around' and a cover version of 'Wishin' And Hopin'', a US hit for Dusty Springfield. By now The Merseybeats had acquired the sartorial elegance they'd demanded of Brian Epstein and came dressed in frilly shirts and bolero jackets. They also acquired some attention from the Sunday newspapers, who revealed that the band expected more from their girl fans than

I THINK OF YOU
The MERSEY BEATS

mere demands for autographs. And so The Merseybeats achieved a modicum of notoriety. Which didn't really do them any great harm.

Nevertheless, it was October '65 before the next real hit came their way. By then they had Billy Kinsley back on the team and also a new management deal in their pockets. It seemed that a revitalised career was in the offing, especially as their recording of 'I Love You, Yes I Do' began climbing the charts. But they released one more single – 'I Stand Accused', in December 1965 – and then packed it in, Aaron Williams and John Banks, who'd suffered a nervous breakdown, deciding that touring just wasn't fun any more.

Kinsley and Crane decided to carry on as The Merseys, becoming a vocal duo and fronting a back-up squad, initially formed by a band known as The Fruit Eating Bears. With orchestral backing they recorded 'Sorrow' and it became a huge hit midway through 1966 – almost as big as 'I Think Of You', in fact. After that, nothing seemed to work for them. Their records gathered dust on retailers' shelves, their management, Kit Lambert and Chris Stamp, became increasingly involved with The Who, and there were also problems with The Merseys' back-up musicians.

Eventually Kinsley opted for life as a sessionman and Crane linked up with a number of other musicians to form Tony Crane And The New Merseybeats, an outfit which, in one form or another, has been doing its bit in cabaret right up to the present day.

'After three years together,' Billy Kinsley remembers, 'Tony wanted to go into cabaret, but I wasn't too keen on that. So we parted and I went into sessionwork. I had a spell in the Jackie Lomax Band and then achieved one of my childhood ambitions by playing with Chuck Berry on tour. After that it was all down to sessionwork again, though I did do a few singles and an album with a band called Rockin' Horse.'

Also during the early seventies he recorded some solo sides for CBS and took part in a Merseybeat revival show that toured the USA. It was in 1975 that he teamed up with a band called Paper Chase to form a pure pop outfit known as

Liverpool Express and once more become a chart act thanks to records like 'You Are My Love' and 'Every Man Must Have A Dream', both Top Twenty discs in 1976. They also had a mini-hit with 'Dreamin'' during the summer of '77 and then the Liverpool Express shuddered to a halt and Kinsley moved on yet again, his most recent venture being with a Liverpool band known as Cheats.

As for the others – Aaron Williams still lives on Merseyside and, when last heard of, was trying to make some headway as a songwriter: John Banks has been working in Israel since the early seventies: and John Gustafson, a fine bassist, has, since his brief stay with The Merseybeats, worked with just about everyone in his role as a sessionman, also getting involved with such seventies bands as Quatermass and Hardstuff, while in 1982 he surfaced as successful songwriter, co-writer of the Status Quo hit 'Dear John'.

But still it's really Tony Crane who continues to keep the Merseybeat flag flying, continually reviving 'It's Love That Really Counts' and 'Wishin' And Hopin'' for the benefit of the chicken-in-a-basket trade. And as long as singers like David Bowie revive songs such as 'Sorrow' and Elvis Costello dips down into his bag of memories to give the kiss of life to 'I Stand Accused', there should be no shortage of customers!

Millie

IT WAS EVIDENT that Millie wasn't forgotten when Bad Manners revived 'My Girl Lollipop' and were rewarded with a Top Ten hit in the summer of '82. The song, originally titled 'My Boy Lollipop' had provided the fifteen-year-old girl from Clarendon, Jamaica with her first British hit back in 1964. Something of a bluebeat boom – bluebeat being an early form of reggae – had developed in Britain at the time, Ezz Reco And The Launchers reaching the edges of the chart with 'King Of Kings'. It seemed that only a nudge might be required to launch a whole new craze. And Millie Small, who'd already had some record success in Jamaica, appeared to be just what was needed.

Chris Blackwell of Island Records was one who thought so. He brought Millie to Britain, provided her with an American song in 'My Boy Lollipop' and had Harry Robinson, of Lord Rockingham's XI fame, to supply an apt backing to Millie's high-pitched screech of a vocal.

Everything went according to plan. The record went Top Five in both Britain and America and little Millie Small, the youngest in a family of twelve, got the whole bluebeat-ska-reggae bandwagon rolling in the right direction. And, though some folk today remember her as a one-hit wonder, the truth is that she had Top Thirty success with her follow-up 'Sweet William', which admittedly would have been hard to distinguish from 'My Boy Lollipop' on a foggy night. Also in 1965 she sold quite a few copies of 'Bloodshot Eyes' too – though nothing like the three-and-three quarter million pressings of 'My Boy Lollipop' that had brought her world-wide recognition.

Her chart-climbing activity behind her, Millie hit a quiet patch for a while, reappearing in mid-1969 when she signed a record contract with Decca and made a single called 'Readin', Writin', Arithmetic' which did about as well as a cat at Cruft's. Apparently, in the interim, according to the press hand-out that accompanied the record's release, Millie had spent her time cutting four albums, doing two world tours that lasted around two-and-a-half years in all, and had also got involved in projects encompassing films, cabaret, TV and radio. The release also brought new photos depicting a very grown-up Millie, dressed in a lacy, mini-skirted two-piece. Quite lovely. Very appealing.

Looks, unfortunately, count for very little in the world of hit records. The new Decca single flopped and, though the cause of reggae advanced throughout Britain, Millie's popularity declined, most of her work coming from the various small clubs up and down the country.

Millie's still doing the rounds today, on the club circuit. A South Midlands promoter explained to me that Millie had been working on his patch for years. 'She's still a very good performer, though maybe one who's now not popular enough to have back within a very short space of time. Nevertheless, she plays each club perhaps once a year and turns in an extremely worthwhile show.'

Nowadays, he added, she's based in Sheffield and is managed by her husband Ron Raymond. So Millie Small has become Mrs Raymond, a thirty-odd-year-old singing housewife with a stepdaughter.

But on the bills she's still 'Little Millie – hit-maker of "My Boy Lollipop". And that, I guess, is the way things will stay.

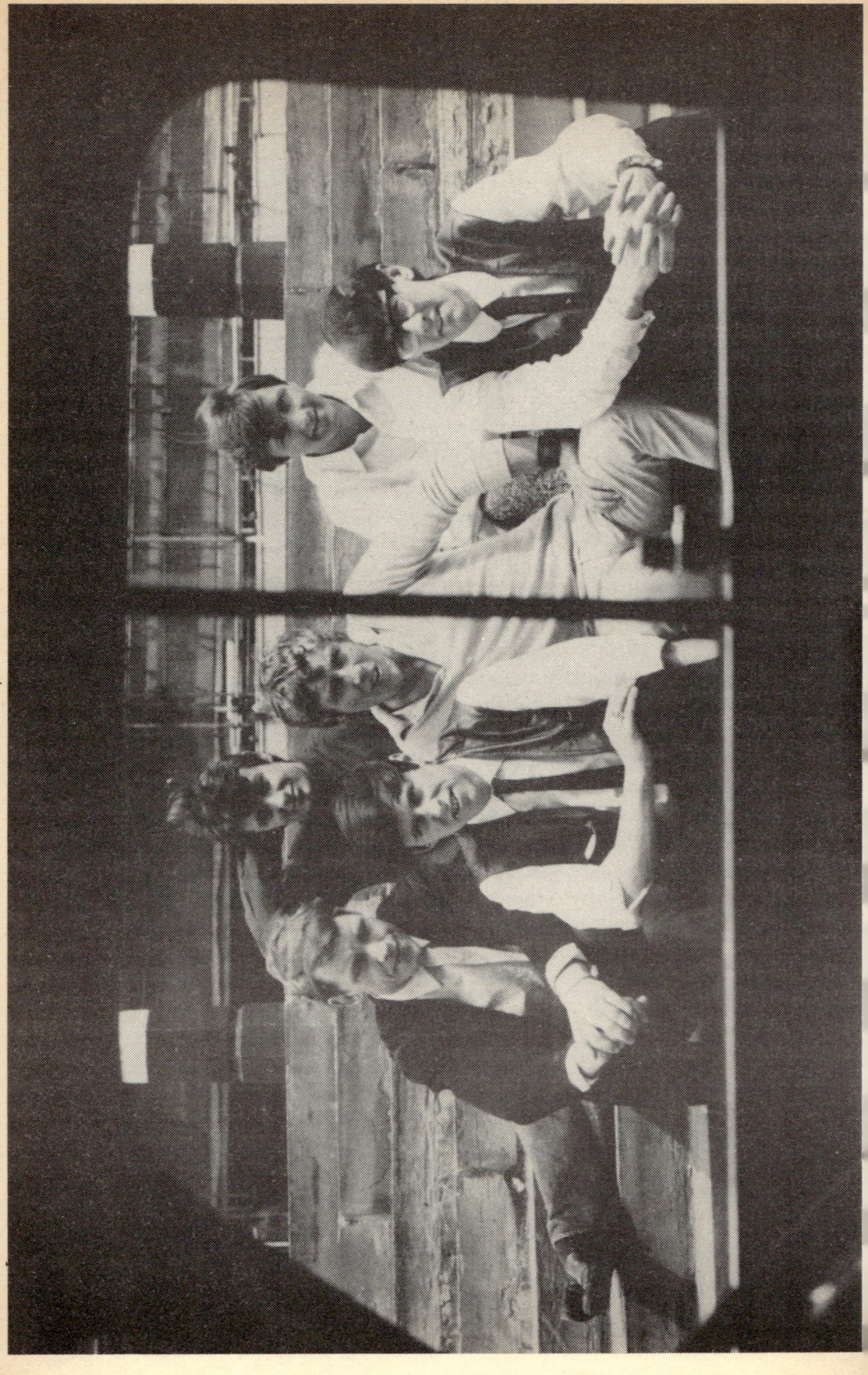

Nashville Teens

Out of stockbroker country they came. Weybridge, in fact. And they dispensed a line in sixties rock that often came both tasty and torrid. Veterans of tours with Jerry Lee Lewis and Bo Diddley, both of whom they backed. The Nashville Teens – Arthur Sharp (vocals), Ray Phillips (vocals, bass, harmonica), John Allen (guitar), Pete Shannon (guitar), John Hawken (piano) and Barry Jenkins (drums) – were managed by Don Arden (now manager of ELO and mainman at Jet Records) and initially produced by Mickie Most, then vocalist with The Minutemen.

'Mickie took us into the studio and went through a few of the things we had, songs like Mose Allison's "Parchman Farm", etc.,' says Ray Phillips. 'Then he asked if we had anything else and we told him we'd been toying around with the idea of recording "Tobacco Road", a number we'd first heard on a John Loudermilk album at the record shop where Arthur Sharp worked. So we did it – everything just went from there!'

The record provided the Teens with their first and biggest hit, blueswailing its way into the UK Top Ten during 1964. They followed it with another Most-produced Loudermilk song, 'Google Eye', ('I personally didn't like it' – Ray Phillips) which again provided the Teens with Top Ten status, along with offers of appearances in films such as *Gonks Go Beat* and *Be My Guest*, plus a month-long trip to the States. While in America, they recorded 'Find My Way Back Home' plus 'Devil In Law', a song brought to the band by Johnny Moore of The Drifters. But the resulting single failed to arouse much interest when it was released in 1965 and also caused a bust-up between the band and Mickie Most, who claimed that the American recording session formed a breach of contract. Further disasters followed when such singles as 'This Little Bird' and 'The Hard Way' failed to make even the Top Thirty and so the Weybridge wonders went back to supporting visiting dignitaries like Chuck Berry and Carl Perkins, playing a glorious London Palladium show with Gene Vincent in 1969, at which they barnstormed their way through a vibrant set which was received with nothing but jeers by the audience of anachronistic greasers.

It's been reported that the Teens broke up in the wake of this fiasco but this simply wasn't so.

'That report was rubbish,' says Phillips. 'We've never been off the road. Unless I've been on holiday or something, I've played somewhere just about every week since the early sixties. I remember that Vincent gig though. The place was full of real old-fashioned rockers and we did things like "Chantilly Lace". But we didn't do the Big Bopper version, we did it our way – and that, I guess, was a bit like showing a red rag to a bull.'

However, though the Teens didn't jack it in, John Hawken left to join a series of bands that included Renaissance, Spooky Tooth and the Strawbs before apparently disappearing off the face of the earth.

Phillips explains: 'John was a funny guy. He was a great keyboard player but had very high principles. If anyone with whom he was negotiating didn't meet up to his standards then he'd knock the whole thing on the head, no matter how much money was involved. Eventually he met and married an American girl who lived just up the road from me. She wanted to go home and John also liked the idea of going to the States so off they went – though I've since heard that they've split up, which is very sad. Barry Jenkins left the band very early on. He went to join the Animals in 1965. But the biggest blow was when Arthur Sharp left in 1972. We were bosom buddies, we'd got together after heading rival bands in Weybridge, round about 1960, and we were Barney Rubble and Fred Flintstone – or Laurel and Hardy, as The Who used to call us. Anyway, Arthur just came up one day and said:

"Look, I can't make it any more. My heart's not in it and I'm getting too fat. Times are bad and when the kid needs a new pair of shoes I just haven't got the money." When Don Arden offered him an office job, he took it. He's still with Don now – at Jet Records. And when The Nashville Teens did the *Heroes And Villains* concert in September, 1982, I met him again for the first time in something like five years.'

In the early seventies, the Teens recorded for EMI, who released none of the sides, and for Major Minor, who went broke just as a single was about to be released. A dispute with Don Arden ensued and this, in turn, meant that the band was unable to record for several years, though Ray Phillips kept the Teens on the road, for a while working with pick-up units before, in 1976, establishing a regular personnel once more.

Currently, The Nashville Teens are a four piece comprising Ray Phillips, bassist Len Surtees, drummer Adrian Metcalfe, and a Hendrix-inspired guitarist named Peter Agate. Phillips says that he's never made any money out of his constant touring but remains happy with his lot. After all, time hasn't dealt him too bad a hand. He looks at least ten years younger than his real age (he admits to being 43 but fails to add a couple of extra years), has an attractive wife, Rosalinde, plus a couple of kids. And if his Addlestone semi is modest in comparison with some of the near-palaces owned by a few of the local superstars, then it's nothing to turn your nose up to. 'It's a hard life,' Ray once admitted. 'People think that because you're on stage it's all great. But they forget you may be up there for just half an hour and then it's back on the road for the next twenty-four. Touring is expensive and I just make enough money to survive. There's no great profit in it unless you're in the charts.'

In mid-1981 The Nashville Teens, after many years, attempted to get into the charts once more with a single called 'Midnight'. It didn't exactly set the world of rock alight but it did glean a fair share of media coverage – if only because Ray Phillips, with tongue-in-cheek, dedicated the record to Don Arden, whose affairs at that time were much in mind due to a BBC *Checkpoint* enquiry. The Teens further capitalised on this by mounting a 'Be Nice To Don Arden' tour, even offering to play a benefit for Arden who, to the best of anyone's knowledge, has never been short of moolah for many years! The tour was no big deal status-wise, the venues ranging from the Half Moon, Putney and the Llanidloes Powys Community Centre through to the London Rock Garden. But it kept the band in the public eye and demonstrated that The Nashville Teens were still playing mainly rock venues and hadn't succumbed to being a pure vaudeville act, like so many. Then, in 1982, came the Hammersmith Concert and great reviews, the release of 'Live At The Red House', a mini-album, which was followed by a Teens' appearance on the 'Heroes and Villains' album and some TV dates that included ITV's *South Bank Show* and Channel 4's *Unforgettable* series. Over twenty years, The Nashville Teens are still heading down Tobacco Road and seemingly not out of puff.

'People often ask me what I'll do when I'm past it,' smiles Ray Phillips. 'But, believe me, I'll just keep on doing what I'm doing until I drop.'

The Pretty Things

NO, THEY WEREN'T a pretty sight at all. Quite the ugliest group on the scene, to be honest. Mothers swooped to activate the off-switch whenever the Pretties appeared on TV. They made the Stones seem like choir boys, though looking at their old album sleeves, it's difficult to see what all the fuss was about. But at the time they seemed real bad. And the rough-tough brand of bluesware that they peddled didn't help their family image one iota.

Maraca-shaking Phil May was the leader. Chubby-faced and long-locked, he spat out songs like 'Rosalyn' and 'Don't Bring Me Down' and the class of '64 loved him. Aided and abetted by the only slightly more elegant Dick Taylor, the Stones' original bass-man, drummer Viv Prince, bassist John Stax and rhythm guitarist Brian Pendleton, May continued to musically threaten the whole British way of life throughout 1965, the band causing riots and controversy wherever they appeared, even causing a question to be raised in Parliament about the depth of depravity inherent in rock during the sixties.

But the Pretties were never really as big as the furore they caused. None of their records reached the Top Ten after 'Don't Bring Me Down', though 'Honey I Need' and 'Cry To Me', did enough to keep the band in the public eye during 1965. However, sales fell away even further during '66 and Viv Prince quit to become a Hell's Angel, Skip Alan taking over the drum chair for a while before relinquishing his place to Twink. The band started falling apart. Brian Pendleton left, his replacement being John Povey, formerly of Bern Elliott's Fenman. A year later, John Stax emigrated to

Australia and another Fenman, Wally Allen, became a Pretty. Depleted but not defeated, the band made a great album for EMI, called 'S.F. Sorrow', the first pop opera and the inspiration for The Who's 'Tommy'. They also made an appearance in the Norman Wisdom film *What's Good For The Goose*, initially being asked to perform one number but ending up with several spots in the movie.

Singles-wise though, the Pretties were a dead duck. Disheartened, Dick Taylor also threw in the towel shortly before the arrival of 'Parachute', the band's 1970 album, leaving Phil May as the only surviving original member.

By the early seventies morale was low and the band felt well and truly down, even though *Rolling Stone* magazine belatedly declared 'Parachute' Album of The Year for 1971.

More personnel changes ensued, along with yet another record label switch, a contract with Warner Brothers providing May and company with the kind of exposure in the States they'd never received before. Initially it appeared that they might make some breakthrough on the other side of the Atlantic – but it was not to be. The Pretties hung on and waited for the next ray of hope. It came in 1975, when they signed with Led Zeppelin's Swansong label.

The *NME*, commenting on the news, declared: 'The group are now managed by Zeppelin handler Peter Grant and if they can't reap some success out of that heavy backing, then they might as well pack up and go home.'

They didn't, so they did. By the end of 1976, The Pretty Things were virtually no more. Phil May set off on a solo career and it seemed like the end of the line. It was during this period that he made some demo tapes, which surfaced in Europe as an album. The reviews were unanimously awful.

Sometime in 1980 Phil May phoned me to explain not only about the 'solo' album – 'it was substandard and should never have been issued' – but also to announce that he was resurrecting The Pretty Things employing a line-up that included Dick Taylor, John Povey, Wally Allen, Skip Allen and lead guitarist Peter Tolson, who'd previously been with the band during 1973–76. Together they made a Warner Brothers album called 'Cross Talk' which, if nothing else, demonstrated that Phil May had actually *improved* as a vocalist. The revived Pretties toured Europe, appeared in a 1981 horror movie titled *The Monster Club* and then planned a venture that would merge ballet with rock.

But, as usual, the Pretties' luck ran out and they disbanded once more.

At the close of '82, I called Phil May to find out just how he and the rest of the band were faring.

'Currently, Skip and I are trying to put together a blues band in the Notting Hill area,' he said. 'I did some tracks in a studio some months ago with a band that included Simon [Fox] from Bebop Deluxe but there's no complete album. Dick still plays with various people when he's not working for the Jean Machine company and most of the others are still gigging, though not a lot's happening. Like many other musicians we'd like to be able to play together on a regular basis but, at the moment, it's financially impossible. If you put a regular band together, then you've got to be able to pay them whenever you're off the road – which means there'll be some weeks when you've got to find ten people's wages for doing nothing. And the only way to cover this is to put up the price of the band for gigs – which, in turn, cuts down the number of gigs you obtain. I know of some bands who just keep on touring simply because they can't afford to stop. It's a bad situation.'

P. J. Proby

'**J**IM PROBY WAS his own worst enemy,' says a musician who knew him well. 'He had this thing about being bigger than both Elvis and Tom Jones and though in my view he could have taken Jones any time he put his mind to it, he proved unreliable and unstable. Even with friends and people who had helped him with his career he was just the same. Jim was really something of an idiot.'

Proby started life as James Marcus Smith, the son of a well-to-do Texas family. He claims that he was sent to military school at the age of nine, after which he became a twelve-year-old dee-jay. During his teen years he once opted for married life and became hitched to a girl named Maryanne Adams. But this attachment, like any other Proby long term involvement, soon fell apart. Around this period too, he adopted the name Jett Powers, sometimes working as a B-movie actor and maybe providing back-ups on recording sessions with the likes of Little Richard. At one point he even provided demo discs for Elvis himself. But his career really took off in 1963 when, thanks to the efforts of producer Jack Good, he arrived in Britain to appear on the 'Meet The Beatles' TV show.

His charismatic performance made him a pop idol almost overnight and when 'Hold Me', the first P. J. Proby record released in Britain, came out in May, 1964, it stormed into the Top Five with alacrity. That same year saw the release of two further monster hits in 'Together' and 'Somewhere' with its stentorian delivery. Jim Proby seemed unstoppable, the biggest solo thing in British show-biz. He began touring and onstage proved even more of a sensation. He gyrated, thrust

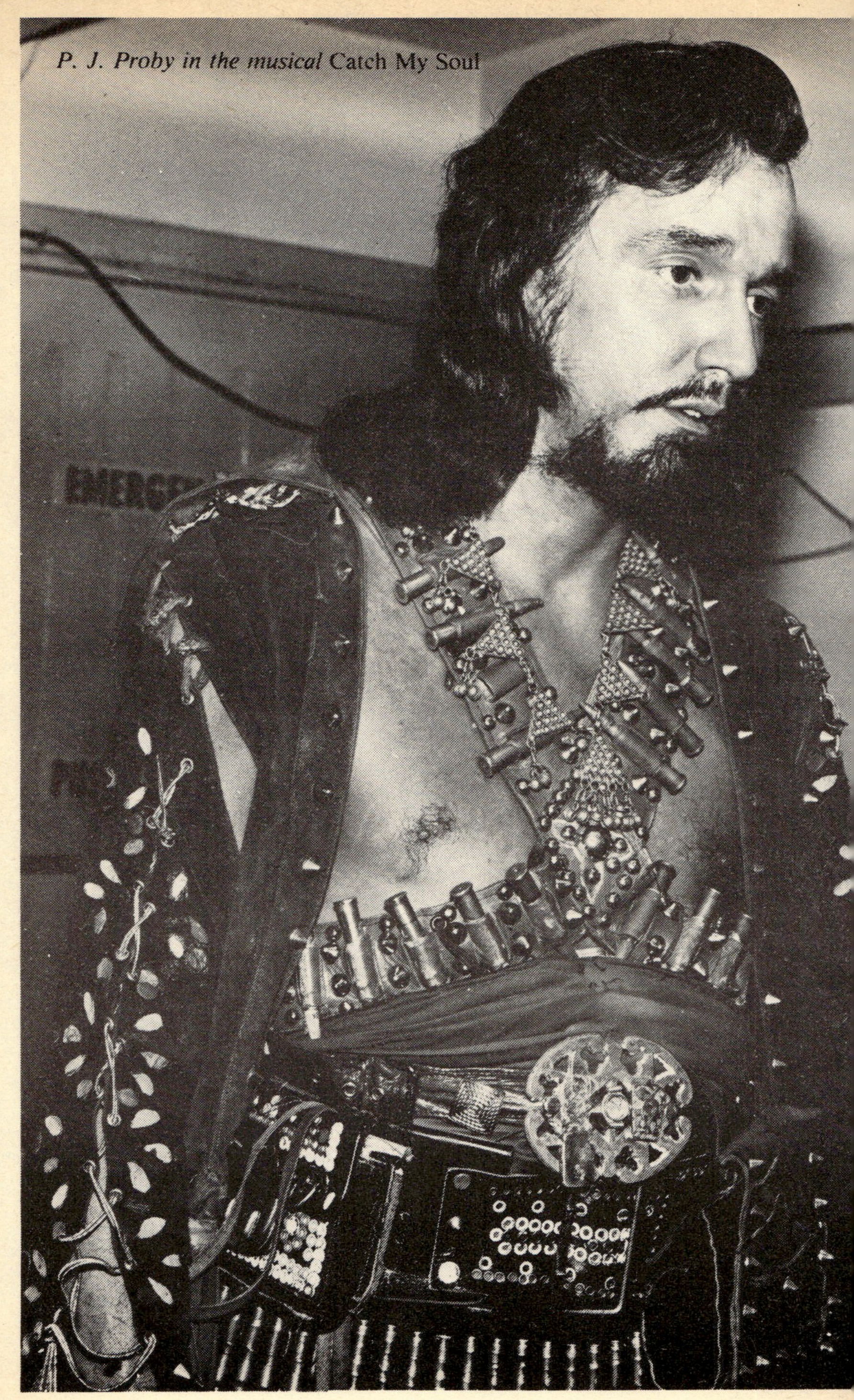
P. J. Proby in the musical Catch My Soul

his pelvis, played the sexual bit for all it was worth. Then, during a Croydon gig during January, 1965, his velvet trousers split right up to his crotch and Jim completed the show holding on to his vital parts. A similar episode occurred at the Ritz, Luton, a couple of days later, and the media unanimously yelled 'obscene!'. Immediately he was banned by the ABC circuit and, shortly after, given the elbow by BBC-TV.

The Proby response was simply wonderful. He put out a version of the old Billy Eckstine hit 'I Apologise' and was rewarded with another massive hit. And throughout '65 and '66, the controversial Texan continued to supply a flow of chartbusters, his final Top Ten single being 'Maria', yet another winner culled from the score of *West Side Story*. Then came the downhill slide. He began logging massive debts in Britain and opted to return to the States where his recording of 'Niki Hoeky' had just provided him with his biggest-ever success in his own country. But he could supply no follow-up and, for a while at least, it seemed that P. J. Proby was no longer a headline grabber.

When he appeared as Cassio in Jack Good's *Catch My Soul*, a rock opera version of *Othello*, staged during 1970, little attention was roused. Then in 1973 he became engaged to Claudia, Dean Martin's daughter and, obviously not too enamoured with having Dino for a father-in-law, was shortly after imprisoned for three months for totin' a shotgun in public. Hits or not, Proby seemed determined to stay in the public eye.

A return to Britain, where he'd been declared a bankrupt (owing £85,000 and having assets of £10!), brought little respite to the flood of controversy. He signed a contract with Ember Records and then claimed that, after a disagreement involving the use of certain backing tapes, he'd been threatened with a spot of the instant harm to his personal well-being. Like maybe a broken rib or two. Departing quickly once more for what he considered the comparative safety of the States failed to slow down the rate of disaster. Ever the Muhammad Ali of rock, he began recording a song called 'The Champ' during 1974. Somebody up there didn't like him though. When leaving the studio one day, he and some of the studio employees were attacked by a gang, and one person was left dead.

In early 1978, Proby, in the constant company of a lady named Dulcie, came back to London to renew acquaintance with Jack Good once more and was signed to become one of the three singers portraying Elvis Presley at various stages of his career (one of the others was Shakin' Stevens) in Good's West End presentation *Elvis*. As usual, given an appreciative audience, he was great. He even won an *Evening Standard* Musical Award. Then nightly routine got to him. He deviated from the script and began chatting to the audience much in the manner that Elvis himself did during his Las Vegas shows. By now his ego was bigger than the show itself. Proby simply refused to revert to the original script and was sacked. Thus his long-standing association with Jack Good came to an end.

Could the enigmatic Proby afford to lose any more friends? Apparently he could. Not long after the *Elvis* debacle he got involved in a fist fight with an American TV director who was trying to help him. Then he was hauled in front of a judge once more after thumping his secretary, Pamela Baglow, and only narrowly missed being hauled before the court once more after firing an air-gun at the long-suffering Dulcie.

These days, P. J. Proby would appear to be once more at the bottom of the heap. But few would give you odds that we've heard the last of him. As Nik Cohn once wrote: 'Proby is the great doomed romantic showman of our times.'

And, along with Scott Walker, I guess he is.

The Rockin' Berries

WHEN IT CAME right down to it, I really couldn't remember too much about The Rockin' Berries. Certainly I recalled their version of 'He's In Town', all high harmonies and easy on the ear, being played to death on the radio during '64. But that was about the state of things. Like finito! However, the Berries did make their contribution to the beat group bonanza of the mid-sixties and, with a somewhat different line-up, are doing very nicely on the club circuit today. There are those with better memories than I. The Rockin' Berries – Clive Lea (vocals), Geoff Turton (guitar), Chuck Botfield (guitars), Roy Austin (bass) and Terry Bond (drums) were a Brum Beat outfit who first got together in 1961. Like hundreds of others they played rock'n'roll cover fare, did their versions of hits made originally by the likes of Chuck Berry, Little Richard and Elvis, and eventually did their obligatory trip to Germany.

They made a couple of nowhere singles for Decca and a moderately successful one for Pye's Piccadilly label. Then, during a tour with P. J. Proby in 1964, they bumped into legendary pop producer Kim Fowley who introduced them to the Goffin and King song 'He's In Town', which The Tokens had just converted into a Stateside hit. He suggested The Rockin' Berries should cover it and they did, the resulting record going Top Five in Britain and sparking off the band's winning streak.

Early in '65, they had a fair-sized hit again with their rendition of 'What In The World's Come Over You?', a revival of a 1960 Jack Scott hit, after which they crashed the Top Five once more with 'Poor Man's Son'. Realising that

the beat boom wouldn't last forever, they switched camps at an early stage and moved into cabaret, building up an enviable reputation as a club act, full of slick routines, impressions and other bits of show-biz. There were still a couple of minor hit records to come, namely 'You're My Girl' and 'The Water Is Over My Head' but, to quote Geoff Turton, the man who provided the distinctive falsetto vocals on the band's early recordings: 'In 1967 we reached the peak of our popularity when we appeared at the Royal Command Performance in London.'

It was Turton's swansong with the group. In 1968 he went solo, changed his name to Jefferson and, shortly after, came up with an enormous hit in 'Colour Of My Love'.

'I was having personal troubles with the group, but when I left I found it was all me. I had two single successes in the States but never went over there to exploit them, which was really an oversight of management. At that time I had a terrible emotional upset with my family and the result was that I angled my despair into songs. And of course, these songs were not suited to my act as it stood – cabaret – so I had to change my whole outlook on life and music.'

Eventually Jefferson did make it to the States, where his second hit 'Baby Take Me In Your Arms' had proved a Top Thirty entry. He gigged around colleges and coffee houses for eighteen months then returned in late 1972 to sign a new recording contract, for Philips, and embark on yet another stage of his career. Since then there's been little news of him, though he still keeps in contact with his ex-buddies in the Berries.

Chuck Botfield's the only original member with the Berries these days, though Terry Bond is still around, having moved into the band's managerial seat. Sometimes, he says, he regrets that early decision to move into cabaret.

'I think all that comedy held us back recordingwise and sometimes I feel that things could have been handled a lot better. The Ivy League wrote "Funny How Love Can Be" for us. We wanted that to be the follow-up to "He's In Town" but the record company just didn't see it as a single and it merely ended up on our album. The reason that we didn't achieve tremendous popularity in some European countries, like many other bands have done, is because we didn't concentrate on the recording side of things. The trouble was that though we had great harmony vocals, it was our comedy aspect that people always picked up on. So we began doing summer shows and suchlike far too early. Anyway, we're still around so things couldn't have worked out too badly. Nevertheless, though cabaret is our bread and butter, we'd still like to make a good record, get a good song. Currently we make our own albums and sell them at shows, like many other acts do.'

Bond still sees Geoff Turton from time to time. 'He was in Birmingham only last weekend. He still does a few gigs as Jefferson though he's mainly concerned with running a hotel business in Littlehampton these days. Clive Lea, who was our impressionist, is now with The Black Abbotts – he joined them as a replacement for Russ Abbott. Me – I went into management about five years ago, my replacement with the band being Keith Smart, a tremendous drummer, who used to be with Wizzard. The management company we've got now not only looks after the band but after other acts as well. So I never play with the band any more – I'm too tied up with office work. Geoff Turton has been back with us from time to time though – I think he's been back about ten times altogether – he even came back after having his two big hits in America.'

At the time of writing, The Rockin' Berries are playing a summer season in Blackpool – 'It's the Berries' show, which we're doing with Bernie Clifton. We're there through to the beginning of September. Then it's back to the clubs again and also the new market we've found in places like Bahrain and Dubai – we're going out there this year.'

The Searchers

T HE SEARCHERS ARE among the ones who never really went away. True, they had their last real hit with 'Take Me For What I'm Worth' way back in 1965. But when the eighties rolled in they were still grabbing features in *NME*, *Melody Maker* and other music papers purely on musical ability and not just as part of some 'whatever became of these boring old farts?' type of article.

Originally they came from Liverpool and formed part of that first wave of groups who provided Merseybeat mania. And The Searchers were as big as many and even bigger than most. There was simply no messin' with them. Their first single went slap-bang to Number One and they were home and dry – just like that. The record that did it was 'Sweets For My Sweet', a cover of an American hit by The Drifters.

One way or another the song did pretty well for a lot of people. Undeniably it enhanced the bank balance of writers Pomus and Shuman. But it also made The Searchers – Mike Pender (lead guitar), John McNally (rhythm guitar), Tony Jackson (bass) and Chris Curtis (drums) the sort of pop personages who got mobbed at every stage door they ventured through. That same year, 1963, they made Number Two with 'Sugar And Spice' and in '64 they challenged even The Beatles in popularity as both 'Needles And Pins' and 'Don't Throw Your Love Away' topped the charts in the UK and 'Love Potion No. 9' proved a monster in the States. Even though Tony Jackson nipped off to form his own band, his replacement being Frank Allen, it made little difference. The Searchers had established a sound of their own – all high harmonies and jangle guitars – and everybody fell over

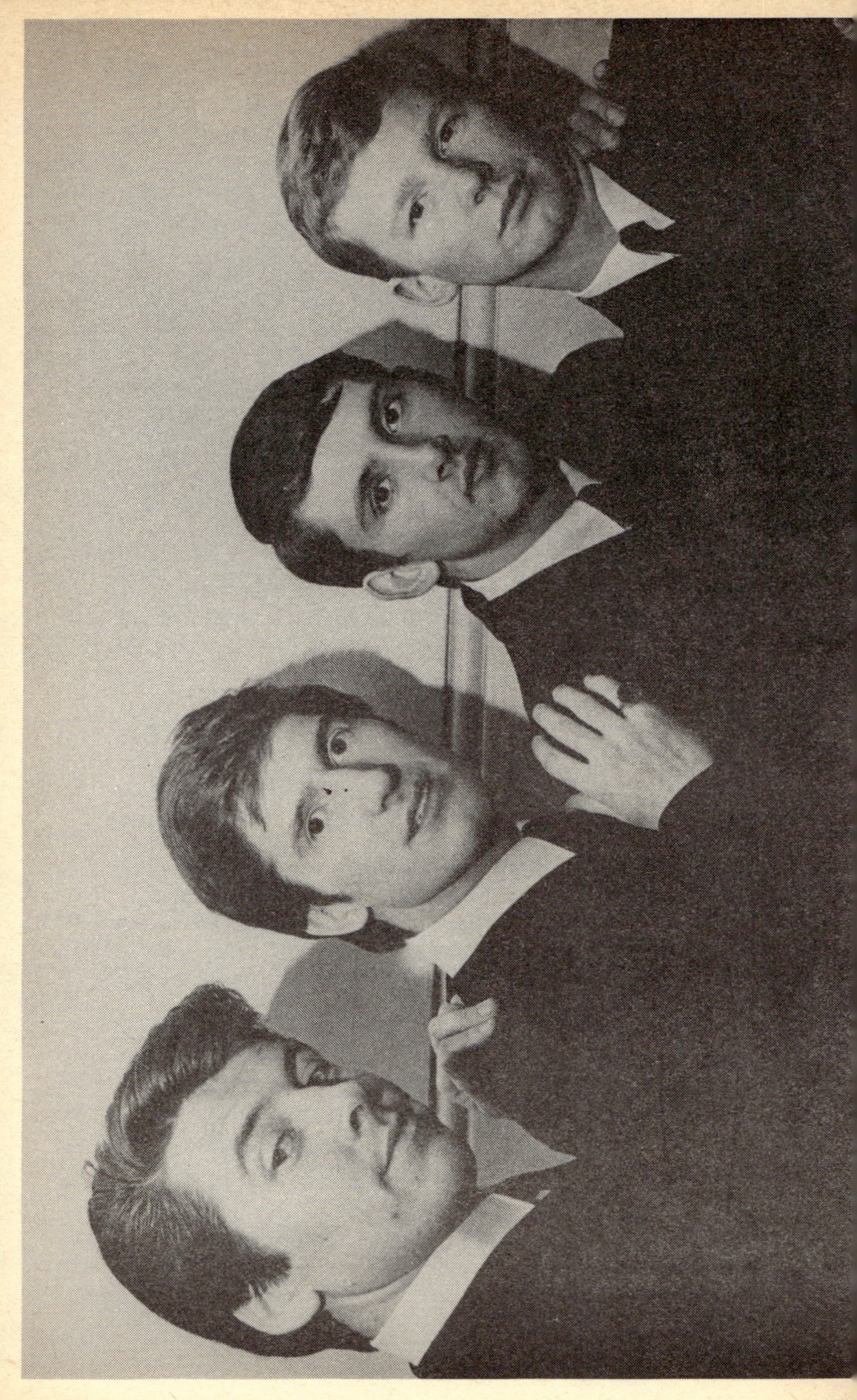

themselves buying their records. So, for a while at least, singles like 'When You Walk In The Room', 'What Have They Done To The Rain?', 'Goodbye My Love', 'He's Got No Love' and 'Take Me For What I'm Worth' continued to provide The Searchers with regular access to the British Top Twenty. It was in 1966 that things began to taper off. The band's singles logged increasingly lower places in the charts and the situation wasn't helped when founder-member Chris Curtis decided to head off and form Roundabout, a group whose members included Jon Lord and Ritchie Blackmore, later of Deep Purple fame. A new drummer, John Blunt, was added and The Searchers continued on their way – albeit at a lower level. Pender and McNally claim that one reason for the band's decline was that they had become totally bored with the pop scene at this point and wanted to spend more time with their families. 'We just got out of touch,' says McNally. 'Everything changed so quickly and we just never kept up with it.'

In 1969 came another change of personnel. Johnny Blunt left and was replaced by Billy Adamson. Amazingly, there have been no team changes since.

With a stable line-up and a collective will to succeed, The Searchers faced the early seventies with no little confidence. They were never without a full work sheet on the club and cabaret circuit and further record deals had materialised. A stint with RCA resulted in a single called 'Desdemona' which nudged into the lower reaches of the American charts during late 1971. Also they were lined-up for the odd overseas tour and even an occasional major concert – like the British Invasion Reunion Show, which played at New York's Madison Square Garden in 1973.

As a result, The Searchers never fell below the poverty line – though McNally and Pender did receive a shock when they were asked to pay surtax bills amounting to £4,000 each – the result of a debt they thought had been settled some years earlier.

And, as the eighties arrived, they became the darlings of the pop press once more, following the release of an album they had made in 1979 for Seymour Stein, the boss of Sire

Records, who had always regarded the band as one of the major influences in rock.

When the album, merely called 'The Searchers', arrived, the media went mildly potty. The music press praised the disc and set up interviews immediately – some held in places where The Searchers were playing, like the Rhydyfelen Non-Political Club in downtown South Wales! The foursome also found themselves playing a number of TV spots for the first time in years.

For a while it was confidently predicted that The Searchers would climb back among the league-leaders once again.

'The passage of time has benefited The Searchers inasmuch as they've learnt to apply their well-hacked licks to more diverse material, the results being both effective and distinctively Searcher-ed' wrote Mark Williams in *Melody Maker*. Another album, 'Play For Today', should have proved the clincher.

But nothing happened.

'Basically, I think it was merely that the band weren't all that interested in making the switch back to the major concert circuit once again,' claimed a Sire Records representative. 'They'd found such a lucrative niche on the club circuit – one that guarantees them three hundred days work each year, if they need it – and they just weren't prepared to give that all up.'

So The Searchers carry on carrying on in their own chosen way – in early 1983 they celebrated twenty years at the top with a concert at Croydon's Fairfield Hall – and McNally and Pender continue living quite happily at their homes in Blundellsands, a seaside resort between Liverpool and Formby, where the air is obviously therapeutic.

I mean, it has to be, hasn't it. For the twosome haven't changed all that much physically since the days of 'Sweets For My Sweet'. Which points to something a little more potent than Phyllosan being involved.

Helen Shapiro

S HE'S NOW CONSIDERED one of the older generation – one of those who made it before Beatlemania set in. Not that she's *that* old. I mean, she's four years younger than Paul McCartney. It's just that winning through early in life can sometimes have its disadvantages.

A Bethnal Green schoolgirl who took singing lessons from a swing-era drummer, Helen Shapiro was fourteen when she made her first record for EMI. Possessor of a somewhat masculine voice – at school she'd been dubbed 'foghorn' – she was presented with a song called 'Please Don't Treat Me Like A Child' at her EMI recording debut. It was an apt choice. How could you treat her like a kid when she sounded as if she'd been thirty all her life?

Not only did she sound different, she looked good too, especially when she ditched her gymslip for an evening dress. Everyone was impressed, the kids, the grown-ups. It would have been hard to set up an anti-Shapiro lobby.

The result was that 'Please Don't Treat Me Like A Child' quickly rose to Number Three in early 1961 and acted as an advance warning for two Number Ones – 'You Don't Know' and 'Walking Back To Happiness'. The following year brought two more major hits in 'Tell Me What He Said' and 'Little Miss Lonely' plus a couple of lesser chartnudgers and Helen Shapiro, bless her bouffant hair-do, was indisputably queen of British pop.

In December '61 she'd been allowed to quit school early so that she could begin work as the female lead in Dick Lester's film *It's Trad Dad*. Actually it was sad, dad, and Helen's acting, such as it was, didn't exactly get her among the year's

Oscar nominees. She sang well enough though, and her career didn't suffer in the slightest. In fact she was offered a further screen appearance in Michael Winner's *Play It Cool*.

For her, things began falling apart in 1963. She began a headline tour of the country but had the misfortune to have an act known as The Beatles further down the bill. As the tour progressed, so things got worse. It was the period during which The Beatles were breaking to become the biggest thing in the whole damn music world and increasingly the audiences screamed each night for John, Paul, George and Ringo, with the result that the tour finally became their triumph.

It was the beginning of a new era – and one which was to reject Helen Shapiro as 'old hat' in the record stakes, even though she tried hard to retain her popularity among the younger generation, recording 'Misery', a song that Lennon and McCartney had written especially for her, and attempting various other ploys.

Nothing worked, however, and though Helen continued to pull in the customers on theatre and club dates, she was never destined to have another Top Twenty record. Throughout the late sixties and most of the seventies she concentrated on club dates and overseas tours, some of the latter being hugely successful. There were also a number of 'one off' recording dates for labels like DJM, Magnet and Arista, none of which managed to re-establish her as a major record artist even though they proved she was singing as well as ever and wasn't immersed in the type of sounds that had first brought her to fame. By the close of '78, she'd had enough.

'I was fed up with doing the clubs. Most of the good ones had closed and at the ones that remained it was merely a matter of going on and repeating all my old hits time after time. If I did anything contemporary, nobody was particularly interested. And so I got really depressed because I was just banging my head against a wall. I was on the verge of quitting the business and it was only after a long discussion with my manager that I decided to hang on and have a go at the theatre. I had done a little bit of acting here and there before and enjoyed the experience. But before we even got down to working out any real plan of campaign, I got a phone call asking if I was interested in appearing in a show called *The French Have A Song For It*. I thought, somebody up there is listening to me after all! Not that the show did particularly well, for it opened and closed quite rapidly at London's Piccadilly Theatre. Nevertheless, it was good for me because it provided me with a real entrée into the theatre and I got great reviews from it. After that, I did *How To Succeed In Business Without Really Trying*, which ran for a few weeks at Bromley's Churchill Theatre, after which came *Oliver*.'

Helen's performance as Nancy in the 1979 West End revival of *Oliver* proved something of a revelation. Ecstatic reviews poured in and Lionel Bart, the show's writer, bored everyone silly with his praise for her contribution to the production. She stayed with the show until the end of its run. After which she 'rested' for a while.

'The reason was that I was turning down clubs and there wasn't a lot of theatre work at the time. Since then I've done panto and toured in a Mike Leigh play called *Goose Pimples*. Mike wrote *Abigail's Party*, which is a wonderful play, and *Goose Pimples* came out of that same sort of improvisational stylistic mould. The part had a lot of character, very open to improvisation, and it gave me a good opportunity to do some straight acting, a kind of method acting, if you like. We did a long tour with that play, since which time I've been up to Oldham to appear in another show. On the recording scene things have looked brighter too. Charlie Gillet, who runs Oval Records, came across a demo record that I did on a song that I wrote with my brother. He liked it so much that he asked me to record an album for British release – the first since 1965! It's a full-of-standards thing, packed with songs by composers like George Gershwin and Harold Arlen – there's only one original song on it. But it's not a cabaretish, big-band, belt-belt kind of affair, packed with done-to-death songs. None of the songs are the sort that have been done-to-death and they've all been given a modern treatment, though they're treated with respect for what the composer originally had in mind. There's basically a jazz feel about things.'

It seems that Helen Shapiro, for the first time in years, is happy with the way things are heading. She feels that she can now build an acting career alongside a renewed music career, establishing the sort of balance that'll eliminate the old frustrations. Which isn't bad, dad.

Sandie Shaw

AFTER CATHY MCGOWAN, Sandie (Sandra Ann Goodrich) was *the* female mod. A short-sighted, singing drainpipe, who paraded the *Ready, Steady, Go!* stage in bare feet, she didn't really have much of a voice. Sometimes the song went one way while her voice tried to head off in a different direction. But things invariably came out all right in the end. The boys thought her sexy and the girls acknowledged her vulnerability. So her records sold in droves.

Originally, she'd been a punch card operator at Ford's Dagenham plant. Legend has it that she appeared at an Adam Faith gig one night in 1964 and began singing in the next-door dressing room. At which point Adam discovered her, introduced her to his manager Eve Taylor and from then on . . . well, you know the rest.

She teamed with songwriter Chris Andrews but the first record resulting from the alliance flopped. Then she did a cover version of Lou Johnson's 'Always Something There To Remind Me', which not only achieved total chart domination in Britain but also sold equally well as the original Dionne Warwick version in the States. During '65 and '66 Sandie continued piling up an imposing tally of hits, often using Andrews songs, the most potent of these being 'Girl Don't Come', 'I'll Stop At Nothing', 'Long Live Love', 'Message Understood', 'Tomorrow', and 'Nothing Comes Easy'. In 1965, she sang 'Puppet On A String' at the Eurovision Song Contest and, despite being technically outsung by most of the opposition, made everyone else seem like non-starters.

Off-stage, the myopic cockney proved she could be as

much a hellraiser as anyone else in the world of show-biz. She moved from scrape to scrape, got herself into the Sunday papers and didn't seem to give a damn. One divorce court judge even described her as 'a trumped-up little cat'.

Then in March, 1968, she married designer Jeff Banks and settled down to semi-domestic life, still cutting the occasional hit, such as 'Monsieur Dupont', a 1969 biggie, but gradually working less and less. She had a daughter named Grace and took time out to announce to the world at large that 'My first baby is my last. Quite a few middle-class people are aware of the population explosion.'

During the early seventies, housed in a luxury home at Blackheath, Kent, she did a few weeks in upper-bracket cabaret each year, helped her husband on the advertising side of things and, when at a loose end, indulged in bouts of water-colour painting and games of scrabble.

'I was a scatterbrained 17-year-old who didn't know about anything,' she admitted in one interview. 'But you grow up pretty fast in pop music, I can tell you. You get to twenty-five and you've seen a lot of things in a lot of places. I used to scream and shout when things upset me – "Sandie Shaw In Airport Scene", all *that* kind of thing. But being married to Jeff has helped. Now I'll probably get near to blowing my top but instead go outside and sit in the garden quietly until the whole business blows over.'

Though the hit records had dried up in 1969, every now and again she'd try and remind the world of music that she was not only around but had also moved on, once or twice fronting a rock band with some distinction. But it seemed she was fated to remain part of nostalgia, the barefoot princess of pop, forever faced with the prospect of meeting strangers who greeted her with the immortal words: 'Hello, Sandie, how are your feet these days!'

And gradually, as the seventies wore on, she slipped from public sight. She also slipped out of Jeff Banks' life too; by the end of the decade her marriage was over and Sandie was to be found working in a Soho hamburger joint.

In 1982 she surfaced with some impact, initially turning up as a featured vocalist on 'Music Of Quality And Distinction', an album by BEF, a duo who had broken away from The Human League.

BEF's Martyn Ware, in an interview with *NME* explained: 'I think Sandie Shaw is still a respected figure even though it's so long ago that she had her hits. She deliberately left the music scene for nine or ten years and we were lucky because she was just looking to relaunch her career. She's a fairly strange character and not what you'd expect. We were searching for ages for the right song for her to do.'

Another reason that Sandie made the headlines during that year was that she'd moved in with video-king Nik Powell, once an exec with Virgin Records, BEF's record label, and was expecting his baby.

Just a few weeks before the baby was born, Sandie, aged thirty-five, married Nik Powell at a Buddhist wedding ceremony. It was just prior to the ceremony that a *Daily Express* reporter reminded Powell of Sandie's 'population explosion' comment, made during the early seventies.

Puzzled, he explained that he and Sandie had never discussed any such problem. 'Let's just say that she's had time to change her mind,' he said. Predictably, alongside the statement, the *Express* printed a picture of Sandie's feet under the caption 'footnote'.

Some things never change.

The Springfields on Thank Your Lucky Stars

Dusty Springfield

I DIDN'T RATE Dusty very highly at first. Convent girl makes good – that seemed to be about the state of things.

After all, who'd have backed a gingham-clad folkie named Mary O'Brien to become Britain's most glamorous and most soulful singer? William Hill's would have laid odds of 10,000–1.

Born April 16, 1939, in North Hampstead, London, to parents of Scottish-Irish descent, Dusty spent her initial working life flipping her way through jobs at a record shop and a department store, while also fitting in nightclub appearances with her brother Dion O'Brien (later to become Tom Springfield), who led a Latin-American combo.

By 1958, she'd given up her maracas and moved on to become part of highly successful vocal trio known as The Lana Sisters, even gaining a spot on BBC-TV's *Six-five Special* showcase for new talent. But, after a while, she teamed up once more with Dion, plus ex-Eton public school-boy Tim Feild, the threesome forming The Springfields, an outfit that sounded, as the title of their first album suggested, kinda folksy.

Signed to the Philips label in mid-1961, The Springfields (with Mike Hurst eventually replacing Tim Feild) lorded it over their rivals for a period of three years, winning award after award, also logging five British chart hits, including 'Bambino', 'Island Of Dreams' and 'Say I Won't Be There', plus an American Top Twenty entry with a version of 'Silver Threads And Golden Needles'. By this time, Dusty had become the Springfield to watch. It was her voice that the fans clamoured to hear, her face that had the photographers loading their Leicas.

When she went solo in October '63, it came as little surprise. And when her debut single, 'I Only Want To Be With You' outstripped most of the opposition in both the British and US charts, the pop pundits nodded their heads as if to denote that such a happening had always been on the cards.

From that point on, Dusty did all the right things, making fine records that clicked on one side of the Atlantic or the other – usually on both – her stage and television appearances captivating audiences as she swanned around, all bouffant and black mascara, gracefully flicking her hands hither and thither as she presented her highly personalised version of hometown Motown. Ever a soul freak, I was impressed. To the revered names of Diana (Ross) and Dionne (Warwick), I added that of Dusty.

So too did many others. With the result that from 1963 through to 1968 the panda-eyed Ms Springfield just piled up Top Twenty hits such as 'Stay Awhile', 'I Just Don't Know What To Do With Myself', 'Losing You', 'In The Middle Of Nowhere', 'Some Of Your Lovin'', 'You Don't Have To Say You Love Me' (a UK Number One), 'Going Back', 'All I See Is You', 'I'll Try Anything' and 'I Close My Eyes And Count To Ten'.

Offstage, she was frequently unpredictable. There were reports of tantrums at rehearsals and in the recording studio. While her love of Goon-like humour had a habit of erupting in surprising ways, more than one unsuspecting waiter receiving a cream cake in the face during one of Dusty's forays into a Mack Sennett scenario during mealtimes.

Onstage, though, she sought to be a perfectionist, handling poignant ballads, solid soul struts and a parade of pops with equal aplomb, her professionalism gaining her spots at venues like London's Talk Of The Town, New York's Basin Street East and ritzy spots all over the world. Despite the glitter and the glamour Dusty remained endearingly un-star-like at times, revealing to one reporter that she was not only short-sighted but also had varicose veins, deficiencies many pop queens would have gone out of their way to conceal. One way or another, Dusty became everyone's darling. The mums and dads liked her, the kids adored her.

And it seemed that things would remain like that forever. Especially at the close of '68, when Dusty provided what many believed to be her best single in 'Son Of A Preacher Man'.

It was the record she'd been threatening to make for years, a classic R&B item, made in Memphis with the aid of Aretha Franklin's producers, Jerry Wexler, Tom Dowd and Arif Mardin. A gutsy, gritty, black-sounding record, 'Preacher Man', bless its flurry of southern guitar licks, established Dusty as the greatest white soul singer in the world.

But it was to prove her last really big British hit. In 1969, her next likely contender, 'Am I The Same Girl', a vocal version of Young-Holt Unlimited's 'Soulful Strut', hovered briefly around the lower edges of the charts before nosediving.

Then, at least as far as the British record-buying public was concerned, the party, cream cake throwing'n'all, was over.

She'd virtually stopped working in 1970. Based in America, she'd opted for a life of limited onstage appearances and occasional record dates. Then in April, 1972, she'd upped and worked a season at the Persian Room in New York's Plaza Hotel, resulting in a flood of offers from America's supper club circuit, including a season at Las Vegas.

Following the release of 'Cameo' in 1973, an album which spawned no hits, things quietened down until 1977, when Phonogram decided to reissue a revamped version of Dusty's 1969 'Dusty In Memphis' album. I was asked if I'd like to contribute some sleeve notes if the record materialised.

I intimated that I would most certainly love to do so – but before the project got underway, Dusty showed up at Phonogram to put the kibosh on things. No such album was to be issued, she decreed. Not only that, all of her back catalogue material was to be withdrawn. If Phonogram didn't agree, there'd be no new album. Simple as that.

But in early 1978, Dusty gave a reception at The Savoy to publicise the fact that she had just completed her first album for five years.

Dusty explained that she had left Britain for America because she felt she was being driven into a dead-end pantomime and summer-shows routine and was looking for another way out. In LA she became enamoured of the sunshine and by the childhood fantasy of riding the freeways, after which she had settled down in Beverly Hills, sharing her home with a brace of cats known as Edward-Bear and Moomin.

But why the gap between 'Cameo', in 1973, and 'It Begins Again', the Roy Thomas-Baker produced album with which she hoped to spark off a renewed career in 1978? 'Management problems,' she explained. 'I was with a management company in the States and most of the time they saw me as a sleek chanteuse performing in the nightclubs – which I couldn't see as having much to do with the music business. I was being tugged in two directions. They signed me with a record company and expected me to turn out contemporary pop music and then they got me doing these nightclubs. In the end I came to verbal blows with them because I just couldn't work under those circumstances.'

Dusty also went on to explain that the reason she had requested all her old recordings be withdrawn was that she didn't want to compete with her old image and had, at least record-wise, decided to cancel out the past.

Unhappily, though 'It Begins Again' was an above average album, it sold only moderately well and again failed to provide that all-important hit single. Nevertheless, Phonogram's publicity campaign had worked wonders and Dusty garnered acres of space in the press as well as appearing on a shoal of TV shows, generally making her presence felt. In the wake of all the furore, a full scale UK tour, the first for ten years, was planned for April, 1979.

But ticket sales proved disappointing and all the shows were cancelled except for three dates at London's Theatre Royal, Drury Lane, leaving the singer's backers to announce: 'The support left much to be desired and rather than have Dusty play to half-empty houses, we decided to cancel. It looks as if she left her comeback too long!'

It appears, though, that Dusty still hasn't given up. As the eighties moved on, she switched her home base to Toronto and began planning yet another new career, signing a recording contract with the 20th Century label.

However, as it's now over fourteen years since Dusty last graced the British Top Twenty, the odds appear to be loaded against her success.

The Swinging Blue Jeans in 1983
Colin
Ray

The Swinging Blue Jeans

An AD IN the September 14, 1961, edition of *Merseybeat*, the Liverpool music paper, read: 'At The Cavern next Tuesday (19) – Gerry And The Pacemakers, Remo 4 and The Bluegenes.' That's how Ray Ennis and his mates were known in those days – as The Bluegenes. Not that they were known to a very wide public. In *Merseybeat's* January, 1962 poll they didn't even gain a place among the top twenty bands. Nevertheless, just eighteen months later, the band – Ennis (vocals), Ralph Ellis (guitar), Les Braid (bass) and Norman Kuhlke (drums) by then known as The Swinging Blue Jeans, had an HMV recording contract under their belt and a minor hit, 'It's Too Late Now' to act as a two-fingered salute to those who had ignored them in the past.

But it wasn't quite the overnight success story it appeared to be. The band had formed as early as 1959 and had embarked on the requisite Liverpool-to-Hamburg round trip more than once before being scooped up in the EMI basket as the major record companies made their way through the Merseybeat supermarket searching for all possible challengers to The Beatles.

Initially it seemed that both EMI and The Swinging Blue Jeans might be onto a good thing. The band claimed a regular spot on a weekly Radio Luxembourg show called *Swingtime*, sponsored by a firm of jeans manufacturers, turned up to play a gig in fictitious Newtown during one episode of BBC-TV's *Z-Cars* series, and soon gained second place in the charts, during early '64, with their cover of a Chan Romero hit called 'Hippy Hippy Shake'.

But theirs was a brief – if well publicised – moment of

glory. There were just too many groups around, most of them boasting much the same sound and all feeding off the same supply of American R&B chart covers. Just two hits later – 'Good Golly Miss Molly' and 'You're No Good', the latter a summer monster in '65 – and The Swinging Blue Jeans were virtually pants from the past in terms of record sales.

Ralph Ellis quit and was replaced by Terry Sylvester from The Escorts, a second generation Liverpool band. And it was with this line-up that the band continued on its way for some time playing top-class gigs and even having moderate record success with their version of Dionne Warwick's 'Don't Make Me Over' during 1966.

By this time however, the jean-machine hype was long past and the band, forced to make it on musical merit alone, suffered from not possessing a capable song-writer, virtually all their best songs being covers of other people's material. Their last single on EMI's HMV label came out in August, 1967, and that, to all intents and purposes, was it, as far as life at the top was concerned.

Terry Sylvester went on to join The Hollies in January, 1969, and has not been short of a bob or two ever since, while Ray Ennis has continued leading The Swinging Blue Jeans up to the present day, still constantly reprising 'Hippy, Hippy Shake', which, thankfully, he's still in the right shape to perform. The father of two, in 1981, at the age of 39, he cut a single called 'I'm An Old Rock'n'Roller'. But, he explained, he didn't feel *that* old, and even felt sorry for the kids of the eighties.

'They come up to me and say they wish they'd been around in the sixties – they feel that they've missed out on a great part of musical history.'

Norman Kuhlke isn't with the band any more. He now runs a sandwich bar, while Ralph Ellis was last reported to be holding down an insurance salesman's job. But Les Braid is still with the band today, playing alongside Ennis, drummer John Ryan and lead guitarist Colin Manley, whose pedigree includes a stint with the Remo 4.

Currently they're managed by brothers Ray and Hal

Carter, who claim that The Jeans are never short of work.

'The band are especially big in places like Germany and Scandinavia. They played Denmark five times during '81 and last year spent several weeks in Germany. In 1983, too, they've got a lot of tours lined up, including a European capitals tour on which they'll be joined by The Tremeloes and John Peel. The thing is that half the original band is still there. Some bands don't have any original members any more. The Ivy League haven't had any original members for years – from not long after their hit period in fact. But the line-up they've got now is incredible. They're a comedy band, though they're capable of doing brilliant harmony stuff. We did a tour with them recently and had to work our arse off to get the audience after The Ivy League had been on. We managed to do it though. By the way, did you know that we had Billy Kinsey playing guitar for us in 1970 and did you know we've got a record out in Denmark called . . .'

You can safely say that The Swinging Blue Jeans, adroitly masterminded by Jim Ireland during their heyday, are still not short of enthusiastic management!

The Temperance Seven

Pick up any book about British beat groups of the sixties and, likely as not, you'll find some mention of The Temperance Seven. Daft really, because The Temps were basically a lot of old jazzers who were a little more eccentric than most. A point brought home whenever their ultra-straight, white-suited vocalist Paul McDowell did his impression of late-twenties favourite Whispering Jack Smith and sang through an ever-handy megaphone.

Another funny thing about The Temps was that they couldn't count. They usually had nine members on display, not seven, the reason for this lack of mathematical accuracy being, in the band's own words, that they were 'perpetually one over the eight'.

Hailed as an overnight sensation, which they weren't, The Temperance Seven appeared on *Juke Box Jury* one night in 1961, gave their version of 'You're Driving Me Crazy' and then sat back and raked in the ackers as the record quickly sped all the way up to Number One.

The whole thing seemed a joke. A send-up of twenties jazz-oriented dance music. And for a while the 'joke' wore well. Their next single, 'Pasadena', was another major hit, reaching the Top Five in the charts, while two other releases that year, 'Hard Hearted Hannah' and 'Charleston' both did well-enough, though a tapering off in interest was apparent.

Still the band motored on, having success in other areas. In 1962 they appeared in the film *It's Trad Dad* and upstaged every jazz outfit in the production along with most of the pop performers. They toured on pop shows desirous of a little light relief and did their fill of TV and radio slots, also appearing in the Mermaid production of the Spike Milligan-John Antrobus play *The Bed Sitting Room*. In short, they got around.

Noted jazz buff John R. T. Davies was the band's trombonist during its heyday. Then boasting a fetching line in fez and performing under the pseudonym of Sheik Haroun Wadi El Yadounir he helped mould The Temps into a sixties phenomenon.

'The band originally grew out of The Royal College Of Art. I wasn't in it at the very beginning. It had been in existence for a couple of years in a sort of desultory fashion, when a couple of members called on me and asked if I would arrange for the band. When I first encountered the Seven I would say that the band's music sprang basically from the period 1922–24 and my contribution was to move everything forward about three or four years to 1927–28. Suddenly the music became very acceptable to modern ears. It was then that we became popular, staying a flourishing musical concern until 1963 or '64, at which point the funny hats began to take the limelight and the music a back seat. This resulted, I suppose, from the flow of appearances at clubs where we were billed as a cabaret act. We were always considered funny, right from the start. Not that we were – we didn't think of ourselves as funny at all. We were not making an imitation of the nineteen-twenties music but rather taking the spirit of it. What we attempted to do was to go back in time and create a kind of branch line. Anyway, we did well, appeared in *It's Trad Dad* and did rather better in *Take Me Over*, a sort of Ealing Comedy type affair and apart from doing *The Bed Sitting Room*, also went back to The Mermaid and did another show called *The Royal Commission*, which, as far as I remember, died rather badly. The band also appeared on a TV series with Arthur Haines, Paul McDowell disappearing from the line-up about that time, sousaphone player Martin Fry also leaving during that period. We carried on though – bringing in Alan Mitchell as lead vocalist. We grabbed him from some successful London show. Things carried on then until August or September 1968 when, with music having gone down, most of us were dissatisfied and so the band broke up.'

Sometime later, drummer Dave Mills leased the name The Temperance Seven from the band's original members and set out to conquer the world. But what transpired soon helped to get him blacklisted by Equity.

'The band went out to Hong Kong, where they played for six weeks. At the end of the stay they went to the hotel manager and asked for their tickets for their journey home, only to have the manager look at them scornfully and ask: "What bloody tickets?" After this, there was a run on the British Consulate in order to get home. One member managed to get back by tramp steamer, while rumour has it that another actually hitch-hiked all the way back to Britain! Alan Cooper, the band's original sax and clarinet man, was one of those who embarked on that Hong Kong fiasco.'

Cephas Howard, the Temps' trumpet star during their pop period and one of the four present members of The Temperance Seven Ltd, the company that holds the rights to the band's title (the other members being John R. T. Davis, banjo and spoons wizard John Watson and percussionist Brian Innes) is now running a crafts centre at Arraton, on the Isle of Wight and appeared in the 1982 TV documentary series *The Islanders*. Brian Innes is busy working for Orbis, publishers of the *History Of Rock* partwork, John Watson's a graphic designer in Twickenham – much of his work being for a firm who make the sweets that go into amusement arcade cranes – while Paul McDowell, who left the band 'simply because he got bored with it' has never stopped doing bit parts on radio, TV and films. Just switch a knob and you'll probably find him. Among the others who formed the nontet during their glory days there's Ray Whittam, who has the most incredible story of all. The band's bass and tenor sax-player he went to America where he was found to be suffering from leukemia. 'But,' as John R. T. Davis is happy to recount, 'he didn't die – he's one of the few people who have had the disease and been written off but still have somehow managed to survive. Today he's really fit and well and making music somewhere in Philadelphia.' The Temperance Seven as a band hasn't died either. Currently, drummer Ian Howarth, 'a spotty-faced fan during the sixties' has the band's name on hire from The Temperance Seven Ltd. and, whenever possible, employs any original members seeking a gig.

'I was on a couple of shows last year,' says Sheik Haroun, 'And on one of those gigs we had Will Hastie, while on both of them we had Bob Mickleburgh — each of them were members of The Temperance Seven during the sixties. It was fine working with them but as far as the music was concerned it was slightly disorganised jazz with not a smell of the band's original concept.'

Does he — a record collector with over 14,000 78s in his collection — ever miss working on the same bills as rock and pop groups, as The Temps once did during the sixties?

Apparently not. 'In those days, when our spot was done and the other guys started setting up their thousand-watt amplification we simply fled the building as we had no wish to be deafened. I do owe something to Elvis Presley though — I dropped a test pressing of "Jailhouse Rock" into Sotheby's recently and was staggered to be notified that it had sold for no less than eighty pounds!'

The Tornados

'TELSTAR' PUSHED EVERYTHING else to one side in 1962. Penned by Joe Meek, a 29-year-old studio engineer turned parlour record maker, to celebrate the first transmissions by the Telstar satellite, the number was recorded by The Tornados, a Meek-masterminded group, and immediately grabbed the Number One spot in the British charts, a position it clung to for no less than five weeks. Across the Atlantic, enthusiasm was hardly less subdued. There, the single also became a chart-topper – the first British rock record to do so – and remained at the top for three weeks, while global sales edged towards an incredible five million mark.

Not at all bad for a record cut in a small North London room and featuring a band whose previous major exploit had been backing Billy Fury in a season at Great Yarmouth!

The Tornados – George Bellamy (guitar), Roger LaVern (a keyboardist who'd started life as plain Roger Jackson), Alan Caddy (violin and guitar), Clem Cattini (drums) and Heinz Burt (a grocer's assistant from Southampton who'd learned to play bass) – momentarily threatened The Shadows as Britain's most popular instrumental outfit. 'Globetrotter', a follow-up disc to 'Telstar' did pretty well, as did 'Robot' and 'Ice Cream Man', all UK chart entries during 1963. But it was during this period that German-born Burt, blond-bonced, handsome and the band's most potent visual asset, elected to embark on a solo career, moving on to record a series of discs that included one classic single in 'Just Like Eddie'. Then, as the band's popularity waned and record-buyers became tired of The Tornados highly stylised sound – one dominated by

ROCK SHOP

LaVern's Roxy Cinema organ approach – founder-member George Bellamy also saw the light and decided that it was time to make it on his own.

By the close of 1964, all five of the musicians present on 'Telstar' had left. And though Meek – who committed suicide under somewhat mysterious circumstances in 1967 – continued to record and promote The Tornados using various musicians, no further success was forthcoming, and the final version of the group finally disbanded.

George Bellamy is now forty-two and the managing director of SRT, a thriving independent record company.

'I seem to spend most of my working life at the company's pressing plant in St Ives, Cambridgeshire,' he says. 'We do mainly custom pressing for other people these days. It's something that has increased tremendously in recent years.'

Along the way, he reveals, he's recorded for EMI, worked for the Keith Prowse publishing company, spent a while as a studio musician and back-up vocalist and also led a band in London's West End before electing to form his own record company in 1971. He was also involved in one last attempt to head back to the good times when, in mid-1975, he, Burt, LaVern and Cattini reformed as The Original Tornados and recorded a new version of 'Telstar' for SRT. But though the quartet did their best to drum up interest, employing a brace or three of old fashioned, sixties stunts, nothing came of the venture and all four quickly returned to rather more mundane activities.

Alan Caddy, the only member of the original band not to join in the attempted revival, has been working in music management for several years now. 'But we don't keep in contact with him,' says Bellamy. 'He, for reasons best known to himself, doesn't let us know where he is. But Roger is now back in Mexico (where, in the late sixties, he became involved in the world of advertising), Heinz has returned to Southampton, though I don't know what he's doing, while Clem continues living in North London and remains one of the most highly-employed sessionmen in the country, turning up on *Top Of The Pops* most weeks.'

Heinz, in fact, has been working in a bakery, having moved

to the area from Essex, where he worked first as a potato delivery man and later in the advertising department of the *Southend Evening Echo*.

Roger LaVern once claimed that though the original version of 'Telstar' proved an awe-inspiring money-spinner and one which has been reissued or repromoted more than once by Decca over the years, neither he nor any of the other musicians involved ever received much in the way of remuneration. George Bellamy confirms this. 'Though the record made a fortune, somewhere in the link between Decca, Joe Meek and ourselves, the money seemed to disappear. Certainly Decca paid all royalties, there's no doubt about that. But we received very little – and when Joe Meek died he was penniless. So you figure it out!'

The Tremeloes

BACK IN THE beginning they were Brian Poole And The Tremeloes and hailed from Barking, Essex. Poole, a butcher's son, wore thick-rimmed Buddy Holly-style glasses, which he switched for contact lenses when The Trems decided that they'd forget about being Britain's answer to The Crickets and cash in instead on the Merseybeat boom.

After gigs at Butlins and a regular spot on BBC's *Saturday Club* they gained a record contract with Decca and promptly opted, like many others, to take the easy way out and cover hits that had already been successful for black artists in America. They struck lucky with their version of The Isley Brothers' 'Twist And Shout', which went Top Ten in 1963, following this with a cover of The Contours' 'Do You Love Me?', a release that took them right to the top of the charts, providing Poole And The Tremeloes – then Poole (vocals and guitar), Ricky West (lead guitar), Alan Blakely (rhythm guitar), Alan Howard (bass) and Dave Munden (drums) – with household name status.

For a while the records sold well and the ackers continued to roll in, two more singles, 'Candy Man' and 'Someone, Someone' going Top Ten during 1964. Then sales began to dip and Poole, feeling he could make it on his own, embarked on a full-blown solo career during 1967.

'What happened,' Poole later explained to journalist Steve Turner, 'was that at first The Trems and I started to record separately. We were having minor successes with our joint efforts in '66, but nothing like we had been having, so there was something wrong somewhere. Then The Trems got their record of "Here Comes My Baby" and as it was a hit we

thought it best they split from me and I went out on my own.'

Poole went into cabaret and eventually slumped from sight, giving up the battle in 1970 and once more donning a butcher's apron at E. Poole & Sons, getting into chops rather than pop. A family man, he continued to sing at the odd gig or two, usually reviving 'Twist And Shout' and suchlike. He also recorded from time to time, one mid-seventies venture finding him working with a band called Carousel. More recently, in early 1983, he elected to chance his luck with an outfit named Tramline, announcing a tour plus a new single through Outlet Records. A stayer. That, you have to admit.

The Trems? They lost Alan Howard but enrolled the aid of Chip Hawkes, a singing bass-player from Shepherds Bush.

With Hawkes and Munden handling the vocals, they suddenly found a renewed lease of life as 'Here Comes My Baby', a massive hit, was followed by 'Silence Is Golden', one of the biggest selling records of 1967. They remained remarkably consistent over the next few years, accruing eleven more hits, including Top Ten items in 'Even The Bad Times Are Good', 'Suddenly You Love Me', 'My Little Lady', '(Call Me) Number One' and 'Me And My Life', the last charting in September, 1970. It was at this juncture that The Trems suddenly confided to the press that they considered all their records to be rubbish and that anyone who'd bought them could only be described as a moron.

This ploy proved a wonderful way of not selling records and the many thousands of 'morons' who'd previously been happy to purchase The Trems' flow of rubbish decided to take their lack of taste and accompanying cash elsewhere. In 1971, The Trems made some chart impression with 'Hello Buddy'. But it was really goodbye, Charlie. For it climbed only as far as thirty-five and then departed, gaining the distinction of being the last Trems chart record of any description. 'I don't seem to see The Trems mentioned in the musical press any more,' Brian Poole claimed in '75. And it's true that their activities have sometimes acquired all the aroma of a top secret operation in recent years. But they still continue playing the club circuit, where they're considered a crowd-pulling unit, as their current manager George Austin is pleased to tell you.

'They work every week of the year. This year, among other things, they're off to Malta, Greece, Holland; they're doing the *Video Entertainers* show and they're also recording for CBS once more. They never stop working and, what's more, they're the *only* sixties group in the country that contains *all* the original members – the line-up being Alan Blakely, Dave Munden, Rick West and Chip Hawkes, the same four that recorded "Here Comes My Baby", "Silence Is Golden" and all the post-Brian Poole hits. They're also the same group that played on Christie's Number One single "Yellow River". Christie didn't play on that one, it was The Trems who actually went into the studio, you know?'

I didn't. Though I do now.

The Troggs

R EG PRESLEY STILL remembers the very day when his then manager-producer, Larry Page, handed him the music to Chip Taylor's 'Wild Thing'.

'I looked at the lyrics – "Wild thing . . . you make my heart sing . . . you make everything groovy" – and they seemed so corny that I thought "Oh God, what are they doing to us?"'

But record it The Troggs did, gaining a monster hit. Since when Reg has been forced to snarl the number and add his ocarina solo at every gig the band has ever given. So much for dopy lyrics!

In the mid-sixties, The Troggs were just four of the 18,900 residents who then inhabited the town of Andover, Hants. Reg, a bricklayer whose real surname was Ball, teamed up with Chris Britton (guitar), Pete Staples (bass) and Ronnie Bond (drums) to work the village halls. 'We usually only went about eighteen miles around Andover, taking sandwiches with us. To have gone farther would have been like falling off the end of the world.' It was their records – hurriedly made and raw – that brought both fame and infamy. In the wake of 'Wild Thing' and Presley's own 'With A Girl Like You', a song with an irresistible hookline that went all the way to Number One in 1966, came 'I Can't Control Myself' (banned in Australia and given a restricted play rating by the BBC), 'Anyway That You Want Me' and 'Give It To Me' all somewhat suggestive despite Presley's protestations that he's never sung a dirty line in his life. 'I had a line in "I Can't Control Myself" that went "Her slacks were low and her hips were showing". Everybody took that to mean that the girl's slacks were undone – and that's not what I meant. I was just

writing about *hipster trousers*!' All were hits though as was 'Night Of The Long Grass', which ran into trouble in America because the authorities felt it had some connection with the use of drugs. The Troggs' rough and ready approach to their music didn't help either. They were really the first British punk band. Yokel flavoured perhaps, but still punk.

Funnily enough, they found themselves hailed as flower-power heroes in the States during 1968 when Reg's 'Love Is All Around' became something of an anthem. Then the seventies rolled in and they were nobody's heroes at all.

The Troggs continued to play gigs – because that's what they had always done – and even came up with a record from time to time. But the frustrations came to the fore at one session where the recording engineer in his infinite wisdom left the tape deck on 'record'. Endless four-letter words streamed across the studio as Reg Presley and his mates struggled vainly to get things together. The result was a bootleg tape that gave the band cult status almost overnight. Accordingly, the media developed a renewed love of Troggs and throughout 1973–74, the band received a fair amount of media coverage, Reg revealing in one 1974 interview that The Troggs had only been out of work for two weeks since 1966 – 'and that was through our own fault!'

I met up with Reg Presley in 1976 when I was asked to provide some notes for a cassette called 'The Original Troggs Tapes'. I'd do them, I said, if the tape company would provide enough loot for me to take Reg out to dinner and chat to him – a ploy that proved to be fairly inexpensive for the tape firm because Reg was on a diet and was very wary about calorie intake.

A likeable, if roly-poly, sex symbol, he was still enthusiastic about the band's future – even though, at that stage, Ronnie Bond was the only remaining member of the original Troggs – and claimed, rightfully enough, that he was still making good records.

'I still get lumbered with that "dirty songwriter" classification though,' he claimed. 'Any single I put out now has to be super-clean and gleaming white.'

'But,' he added, 'I love writing songs about the boy-girl bit.

I'm not interested in the 31 bus to Hammersmith or tractors rolling across the field and all that crap. It's okay for people who want to do that but it's not for me.'

At the start of 1983 I phoned Reg for an update on The Troggs' activities. I'd heard that since we'd last met he'd been forced to sell his house, a dream home that he'd built himself. He ruefully admitted as much. 'I had to do it to pay the taxman. One day a demand for £23,000 unpaid back taxes came in and that was it. All part of paying your dues, I think they call it!'

The band had also suffered other setbacks. 'One day we had all our equipment stolen in Marseilles. We went to a restaurant after a show and when we came out all our gear had gone. And it wasn't insured either! Still, things have gone very well for the band recently. We're nearly back to the original line-up – Chris Britton's on guitar, Ronnie Bond's on drums, while our bassist is Tony Murray – and we did an album called "Black Bottom" which is doing pretty well on the Continent. I don't know if it's because of that punk image that people have thrown at us but for some reason or another we've become fashionable again. We did a show at a university up in Leicester recently and it ended up with more people rushing the stage than we had back in the sixties. It was bloody fantastic. We've done a lot of TV recently too – *Unforgettable*, *Carrott's Lib* and a new show for Channel 4. We've kept off the cabaret circuit – we were never that kind of a band – and still the tours come in. In March, we're off to Australia and we hope that we can come back through America. Also we did Dave Dee's *Heroes And Villains* concert at Hammersmith a few months back. That was fantastic, all those bands back together again. I watched everything from the side of the stage and it was great, really great.'

Twinkle

I SUPPOSE TWINKS wasn't very important in the overall scheme of things. She was only a very ordinary singer and didn't have the most memorable of faces though she worked hard to exude dolly-bird appeal. One way or another she made her mark though, upsetting the Beeb and even getting initially banned from *Ready, Steady, Go!*

The reason was a song called 'Terry', a ditty about a biker who, spurned by his girlfriend, zooms off to rendezvous with that great Shell pump in the sky. It wasn't even much of a song. Made you go red with embarrassment for the 17-year-old Twinkle, really. Yet in spite of, or probably because of, all the furore, it revved its way to fourth position on the charts in 1964 and made Twinkle a mini-legend, or a legend in a mini, whichever way you choose to remember her best. Before long the general public was made aware that Twinks, bless her long blonde hair and kinky boots ('I never wear anything except boots' ran one communiqué) had played the national anthem on the piano at the age of three, began singing with a local band at her home town of Kingston-upon-Thames, lived with her parents, who owned twelve cats, and was really named Lynn Ripley, Twinkle being a nickname given her by her sister Dawn.

She meant to succeed. Within days of her first hit record she was out on the road touring with a band called The Gonks. And the public liked her. When her next record, 'Golden Lights', came out in early 1965 it went Top Twenty.

There were a few more records after that, then Twinkle quit the business to settle down with a man called Michael Hannah, her only musical involvement being a smidgen of

songwriting.

The twosome drifted apart but remained friends, Hannah encouraging Twinkle to resume her singing career in 1972–73 during which time she played a small number of concerts and began work on an album.

'That album never did come out, darling,' says Twinks. She called me 'darling' though we'd never met before. 'There was a single but I felt too personally involved with the album to see it come out. It was all about my life with Michael Hannah. He was a wonderful person and I lived with him until the time I met my husband and got married. It was exactly a year afterwards that Michael met his death in that Paris air disaster – just about the time that the album was completed.' So love, death and music played yet another part in the story of Twinkle Ripley. Since that time she's never set foot on another stage.

'I enjoyed doing those last gigs though – I did three with Colin Blunstone. We did the first one at Watford and he was so kind to me, coming onstage at the end of my act and giving me a huge bouquet of flowers. It was lovely of him to do that because it really ruined his entrance later. I did originally plan to keep working but I had two children and though I also had a full-time nanny, I didn't think it right to go on gigging while the children were so young. It wasn't until I made that single for EMI that I felt free again.' 'That' single was Twink's version of 'I'm A Believer', the Monkees' hit, which she recorded midway through 1982.

'It was a bloody vile song. I only did it because I was with EMI for a year and we were still looking for a song. Every time I found a song I liked, they rejected it. One day my manager said to me: "Look, we're going to see this particular person at EMI and whatever song he's mad about, tell him you're mad about it too. At least, that way we'll get a record out." So when this guy said, "I think 'I'm A Believer' would be a good idea," we both said: "Yes, it's the greatest song in the world." I won't say who asked me to do it, though, because he's really a very nice person and one who gave me a good chance.'

Twinks still writes and has plans for further records though she says things will be different next time. 'I've told myself that at this point in my life I must do the right thing and not the easy thing. And I still haven't forgotten that Michael Hannah album. Maybe I'll re-do it one day – or maybe I'll make it into a film – it would make a wonderful story.'

Finally, a word about *those* boots – the footwear which she once claimed she would never be seen without.

'Oh, darling, those boots! The only reason I ever wore them was because my legs were so bloody awful – and they still are. All I really wanted to do was to get into a pair of shoes. God, won't that look awful in print? Still, it's best to own up sometime, isn't it?'

Bloody awful legs or not, I like Twinkle.

The Walker Brothers

Pɪᴄᴋ ᴜᴘ ᴀɴʏ book about British beat groups of the sixties and you'll find The Walker Brothers listed. Which is odd in a way, for the Walkers, none of whom were born to parents of that name, were all Americans who first met in sunny California. Scott (Noel Scott Engel) was the moody one, tall with golden looks and a deep brown voice that fought hard to keep the vibrato in check. Then there was John (John Maus), even taller than Scott but lacking quite the voice and also the charisma. Finally, there was Gary (Gary Leeds), a drummer who appeared onstage as part of the trio but never, for various reasons, appeared on any of The Walker Brothers' sixties records – though this was all kept pretty hush-hush at the time.

The threesome arrived in London in early 1965, played a few gigs, had a flop record and then, in the middle of summer, came up with 'Love Her', a single which established them as a chart act. From then on everything went their way. 'Make It Easy On Yourself', a Bacharach song which Scott handled so emotively you could almost see the hairs on his chest bristle, rightfully grabbed the Number One spot on the nation's charts. The follow-up, 'My Ship Is Coming In', just failed to do so but the arrival of 'The Sun Ain't Gonna Shine Any More' put the Walkers back in the pole position again and Scott, John and Gary became very big business indeed. Further, if slightly lesser hits followed with '(Baby) You Don't Have To Tell Me' and 'Another Tear Falls' and when the Walkers set out on tour in the company of Dave Dee, Dozy, Beaky, Mick and Tich, they got mobbed every foot of the way – even getting banned from a Blackpool North Pier

Scott Walker in the mid-seventies

show because the authorities considered the furore caused by
the Brothers' appearance would create too much of a safety
hazard.

But the Walkers – 'the drunkest group ever', according to
Scott – were, even at that stage, finding that breaking up
wasn't all that hard to do. All three announced solo
projects – Gary actually had a couple of solo hits released in
1966 – and it was no secret that Scott, who, at nitty-gritty
level, really *was* The Walker Brothers, was becoming less
enamoured of his adopted relatives each passing day.
Eventually, things came to a head. 'I've known Scott for four
years and now I can't even talk to him any more,' complained
John. And in May, 1967, following a concert at London's
Tooting Granada, the Walkers split, though they had to
reunite soon after, for contractual reasons, in order to play a
few dates in Japan.

That year, both John and Scott had solo hits – with
'Annabella' and 'Jackie' respectively. Then John faded from
sight, leaving Scott to sweep through the rest of the sixties,
cutting some high-selling albums dotted with doomy, Jacques
Brel songs; enjoying a brace of further hit singles with
'Joanna' and 'Lights Of Cincinatti' and gaining a BBC TV
series that delivered almost as much as it promised.

It's probable that Scott, who in '69 briefly ditched the
Walker nomenclature, could have made his way through the
seventies with just as much success. But he'd always ducked
out of the limelight whenever possible, preferring to hide
himself away in a room where he drew the curtains even in the
height of summer, and the new decade saw him becoming
more of a recluse than ever, his on-stage appearances
eventually being limited to a week at a small Stockport club
each year, where he is said to have picked up a fabulous fee
for providing a set of extremely short duration.

For some time after the Walkers split he continued to live in
London. Later, he moved to Holland and then on to
Copenhagen – 'I'd met this girl, so I went over there and set
myself up and figured that I didn't need all those people in my
face,' Scott claimed in an interview that accompanied the
arrival of one of the solo albums he did for CBS during the

early seventies. 'Now I just come in and make records. I'm not particularly fond of doing live appearances and television.'

It was in 1975 that the miracle happened and the Walkers got back together again. Gary, apparently, had been doing nothing much except making a few demo discs and developing a talent for crafting hand-made filigree silver jewellery, while John, who'd earlier cut some records for labels like Carnaby without success, claimed that he'd been hanging out in the South of France with The Rolling Stones, during which time he'd even managed to kick a drink problem.

Together they made an album for GTO Records, aided by John Franz, the producer of virtually all of their earlier hits and the man known as the fourth Walker Brother. At first it was all Hollywood comeback and then some — there was yet another hit single, 'No Regrets', just to prove the point. But miracles don't last and in the wake of one further album, 'Nite Flights', in 1978, Scott, John and Gary went their various ways once more, Scott turning up at Virgin Records in 1980 to sign a recording contract that, at the time of writing, has not seen him produce even a one-sided single.

In 1982, I was asked to write some sleeve notes for a 'Scott sings Jacques Brel' compilation and tried to contact Scott, who was living in London. It proved a mysterious process, a record company executive having to contact a nameless girl who, in turn, would contact Scott at his hideaway. And though the message was apparently passed down the line, no answer ever came back through the same channel.

A business associate of Scott's claims that Hamilton, Ohio's gift to the world of pop, will emerge with the album for Virgin any time now. 'He also wants to produce a band but doesn't want to get tied-up with anyone who sounds vaguely like The Walker Brothers.'

'It's a long haul back, man, to that dark, dark and dark . . .' Scott mused during one of his last reported interviews. But in 1983 he did make a tentative start on that long haul by working as producer to some Rough Trade recording sessions featuring John Walker and his wife Brandy, who had recently taken up residence in sunny Brighton.

Meanwhile, somewhere in East London, Gary Leeds was involved on a much more routine job and once more reduced to waiting for his own particular ship to come in.

Mark Wynter

REMEMBER MARK WYNTER? Of course you do. You knew him just like you knew the boy next door. Come to think of it, Mark Wynter *was* the boy next door. Well-scrubbed, smartly clad in well-cut suits and as clean and fresh as anything emanating from a TV soap commercial, he seemed to be everywhere during the early sixties. He appeared on every pop show, figured on endless tours, shone out of the pages of girlie mags, music papers and plain dailies alike and figured highly on the list of likely lads approved by the mothers of Great Britain. If America had Frankie Avalon and Tommy Sands, then Britain had their match in Mark Wynter.

Wynter was really quite anonymous though. Ten minutes after his records had been played, you couldn't even remember what he sounded like. No matter, he was an image. And images sold records.

He wasn't always an image though. Once he was plain Terry Lewis, a shop assistant whose singing career began when he was asked to front a band led by a coalman who lived on the same Hertfordshire council estate. Later he appeared at a charity gig and caused quite a stir, eventually moving out to tour with the various package shows and, during 1960–63 began amassing a series of best-selling teen-dream records, most of which seemed dedicated to youthful members of the opposite sex – 'Image Of A Girl', 'Dream Girl', 'Venus In Blue Jeans', 'Go Away Little Girl', 'Shy Girl' and so forth.

Then, just as quickly as he'd appeared, Mark Wynter vanished. 'I ran into bad times and went to Australia,' he claimed later. But pop music's loss proved to be the acting profession's gain. When Wynter returned to Britain he began appearing in a succession of pantos and stage musicals, eventually turning to meatier parts, major success coming when he took over Paul Jones' role in *Conduct Unbecoming*, a Raj-era mystery play that enjoyed a long run in London's West End during the early seventies. From that point on, he's been involved in a number of fine productions, appearing at the 1982 Chichester Festival in both *Valmouth* and *Cavell*, as well as playing the lead in *Henry V*.

Though his pop career is long since over – Wynter hasn't had a successful record of any kind since 'Only You', in April, 1964 – he's never regretted his sortie into the world of pop claiming that it was only his involvement in such forgettable musical screen happenings as *It's Trad Dad* and *Just For Fun*, in which he played the lead, that provided him with a basis for his present profession.

The signs were always there though. Even in 1962, with *Just For Fun* in the offing, he was reported as saying: 'I don't envisage that this movie will give me much scope to really test my acting ability. For, as the title implies, it's a very light-hearted picture with the accent on music and comedy. But I'm very grateful for the opening and it's a step in the direction I'm most anxious to travel.'

Seems that he's since travelled that direction in reasonable style.

The Zombies

SOMETIMES IT'S AN oddball thing that brings a band to mind. And the oddball thing about The Zombies which fans always remember is that they appeared in the film *Bunny Lake Is Missing* in the briefest of spots – on a TV set! – while the movie's trailer featured them quite prominently.

Then, odd things always happened to the Zombies. It was only after they'd packed it in and retired back to the pavilion that they enjoyed one of their biggest-ever hits in the States. They had that sort of luck.

Rock history books show that the band – Rod Argent (keyboards), Colin Blunstone (vocals), Hugh Grundy (drums), Paul Atkinson (guitar) and Paul Arnold (bass) first got together in 1962, Arnold dropping out after the band had observed him playing 'Peggy Sue' with one hand in his pocket at a local gig. After finding a replacement bassist in Chris White, whose father's store in Markyate, near Hatfield, provided an inexpensive rehearsal room, the band then went on to win a *London Evening News* beat group competition and then signed a record deal with Decca, their first single 'She's Not There', penned by Argent, proving a rock classic.

A Top Twenty disc in Britain and a Top Five entry in the States, it wasn't at all bad for starters. But Britain soon turned its back on the Hatfield hitmakers. Perhaps the band's public school/high IQ image didn't appeal to the kids of the day. Perhaps not. The fact remains that though The Zombies could always boast they had fifty 'O' levels between them, they were never able to boast about another British biggie. In America, things were different. 'Tell Her No' went Top Ten

in 1965 and 'She's Coming Home' also sold more than a few copies. The result was three US tours including a Dick Clark Caravan Of Stars spot. Which meant that they were very big indeed.

'There was always an audience to see us abroad,' claims Colin Blunstone, 'and that was good because we didn't have to slog around England doing tattier and tattier gigs.'

However, after a flow of flop singles and one last great album, 'Odyssey And Oracle', Blunstone and Atkinson decided that enough was enough and in 1967 the band folded leaving 'Time Of The Season', a track from their final album, to become one of the biggest US singles of 1969, selling well over one million copies.

Colin Blunstone, he of the breathy voice, gave up music as a full-time profession and went back to his original occupation as an insurance clerk, taking time out to record some titles under the name of Neil McArthur, one of which, a new version of 'She's Not There', was a fair-sized hit in 1969. That same year, after dickering with the idea of forming a new Zombies (in America, several groups calling themselves The Zombies were cashing in on the demise of the original band to the extent of several thousand dollars a night) Rod Argent formed a band called Argent – though he had to wait until 1972 and the advent of 'Hold Your Head Up' before getting back on the chart trail once more. Chris White continued his association with Rod Argent, the twosome forming a publishing company known as Nexus. And though Paul Atkinson and Hugh Grundy initially left the music business, becoming a computer programmer and a car salesman respectively, the twosome returned to find jobs in the A&R department at CBS Records – the very company that had released The Zombies' last recordings.

It was all very incestuous for a while. Atkinson and Grundy were at CBS, Argent signed to CBS and, eventually, even Colin Blunstone decided to make a comeback and sign as a solo artist to the company, his first album, 'One Year', being produced by Chris White and Rod Argent!

From the album came a classy single, 'Say You Don't Mind', a song penned by Denny Laine – and in early '72 it went Top Twenty to be followed, later that year, by the only slightly less successful 'I Don't Believe In Miracles'. Blunstone entered the rock fray once more on a regular basis and began touring. A couple of albums later, however, his career was in tatters once more. Even a move to Elton John's Rocket label in 1976 didn't pay dividends and though he still gained mainly favourable reviews for spasmodic record releases, the general public chose to ignore Colin Blunstone until 1981, when a remake of 'What Becomes Of The Broken Hearted', originally a winner for Jimmy Ruffin, climbed into the UK Top Twenty bringing a modicum of new generation fame to Blunstone and his on-record partner, keyboardist Dave Stewart.

Undoubtedly Blunstone's one of Britain's most distinctive vocalists if one of the unluckiest. 'There seems to be an understanding in this business that I never get any money,' he once complained, no doubt reflecting upon the fact that his years with The Zombies had left him with a bank balance of just five hundred pounds. Right now, if only momentarily, his career is on the upswing once more. Personally I wish him luck. He deserves that much.

Rod Argent's also faring well at the present time. His band Argent went around the rock'n'roll rollercoaster a few times, the highs coming with such singles as 'Hold Your Head Up', a worldwide favourite in 1972, and 'God Gave Rock And Roll To You', which kept the books straight in '73.

The run down the final incline came in 1976. 'I'd had my fill of schlepping my way around the world. Costs had gone up incredibly and we'd come back from a tour of the States very much in debt. All I'd been doing was things with Argent and it'd got claustrophobic. I decided to have a year off from band work — but the one year stretched to a few. I met Andrew Lloyd Webber and did the "Variations" album with him — I work on most of Andrew's sessions now. Then there were other sessions — things like The Who's "Who Are You?" album, a Roger Daltrey album, gigs with Jon Hiseman and Barbara Thompson.

'In 1978 I did a solo album, "Moving Home", in the company of people like Phil Collins and there's been a single,

''Light Fantastic''. The gigs with Jon Hiseman and Barbara Thompson have been great. We did one at Wavendon, John Dankworth's place, and John liked one of my songs so much, he asked if he could have it for Cleo Laine. He also rang me up and asked if I would work on an album with him – we've already done a few tracks. It's been fine doing all these things but now I'd really like to go out with a band on a regular basis once again. Not all the time – but doing maybe three or four months of gigs each year, allowing me time to indulge in all the other activities that I enjoy.'

Amongst the other activities that have managed to keep Rod Argent fully employed in recent years, is the running of a highly regarded keyboards shop just off London's Charing Cross Road, and a similar venture, Rod Argent's Music Store, which is located in the heart of Worcester. He's also written a musical called *Masquerade*, based on Kit Williams' well-publicised book, which made its debut at the Young Vic in 1982.

Argent still bumps into his former sidemen from time to time and says that Chris White is now resident in Spain, where he opened a bar.

'I believe he's now got a production contract with Spanish RCA, which is working out okay. Hugh Grundy, he's moved on to participate in a variety of trades – once he was transporting horses – while Paul Atkinson is currently in America where he's an executive with RCA's West Coast Division. And it was only a short while ago that I ran into Paul Arnold again, for the first time in ages. He lives in Canada these days. He's a doctor there. I remember that he and I were good mates at school and Paul impressed me because, though he never played music, he managed to build his own guitar. He was also the one who came up to me one day and said: ''I know this bloke who sings a bit'' – which is how I met Colin. But Paul wasn't as interested in the band as the rest of us and after that gig and ''Peggy Sue'' – well!!!'